ELEVEN DAYS TO THE PROMISED LAND

AN AUTOBIOGRAPHY AND TIMELY REALIZATION
OF THE PAST AND PRESENT

DINO PAVLOU

with James Farrell

NEWMAN SPRINGS PUBLISHING
320 Broad Street
Red Bank, NJ 07701

First originally published by Newman Springs Publishing 2020

ISBN 978-1-64801-951-7 (Hardcover)
ISBN 978-1-64801-952-4 (Digital)

Printed in the United States of America

To my grandson, you'll always be BRO #1. What a ball to be around you. Thank you for all the delight you bring to my life.

To my daughters, Effie and Olga, and my son-in-law Theodore, it's been the best of times. Here's to many more.

I love you all.

To my old friend Jimmy Weston, you were one-of-a-kind and so are the memories.

Special thanks to James Farrell for grasping the meaning of my story.

CONTENTS

FOREWORD

Without question, *The Godfather* movies have become Hollywood classics, garnering Academy Awards, remarkable box office success, and, to this day, show no signs of aging. Astonishingly, all generations know what you're talking about when you mention these now-iconic and legendary movies.

Eleven Days to the Promised Land is another incredible story in the same vein. In some respects, it is even more dramatic and emotional than *The Godfather* trilogy in that it's all true. Vito Corleone was a fictional character. Dino Pavlou is a 100 percent real, now-distinguished man living in New York. He's an immigrant who survived insurmountable odds in World War II and civil war-torn Greece. What makes this story unique and heartbreaking is that he was only ten years old when he witnessed the atrocities carried out on his fellow countrymen, including his parents. In some cases, the story takes on disturbing and gut-wrenching twists and turns.

Eleven Days to the Promised Land has many lessons of value rooted deep within the story. As a young child, Dino was put through extraordinarily demanding circumstances. He was used with other children as a human shield by Greek communist guerrillas and ultimately comes face-to-face with his adult enemies who destroyed his childhood. To then grow up and accomplish what he did in America is astounding.

Immigrants all over the world will be inspired and reminded of what it took to get them to retain their culture and adapt to their new countries of promise. First-generation Americans, Australians, Canadians, Brits, etc. will adopt newfound respect toward their forefathers when they come to realize the hardships and sacrifices it took to get them there.

Unfortunately, coming to America didn't solve all Dino's problems. A new set of troubles plagued him, including the betrayal from his family and friends in the motherland. Amazingly, he finds true friendship, loyalty, and solace in his adopted country through many renowned celebrities. With the same human spirit and courage that he was able to defeat his enemies as well as his demons, Dino rises above all challenges determined, steadfast, and strong.

It's hard not to be drawn in and go through an array of emotions with his story. Anger, passion, admiration, respect, extraordinary courage, and overwhelming love are emotions that will be difficult to contain.

This story presents us with an exceptionally different type of hero. No matter how many times life threatened him repeatedly with anguish, he fought back tenfold. Unlike fictional superheroes, Dino doesn't have any magical superpowers. All he has is his spirit, his courage, and his wit, which, throughout the story, are almost taken from him.

This is a story that should be told. It will touch the hearts and minds of millions, and to those of us who were fortunate to never have gone through what Dino went through, a feeling of gratitude and respect is inevitable.

Mostly, it's the story of a simple and innocent child who has no choice but to very quickly become a man, fight a remarkable set of turbulent circumstances, and triumph over everything and everyone that dared to strip him of his dignity and integrity.

Jim Dailakis

ENDORSEMENTS

Eleven Days to the Promised Land is a perfect embodiment of the American dream. Only in America could an impoverished boy from a war-torn country grow up to run with the Rat Pack. Dino's journey is riveting, and it unfolds like a modern-day odyssey.

—Mildred Iatrou Morgan
Motion Picture sound and dialogue editor, Hollywood
2016 Oscar nominee for movie *La-La-Land*
2018 Oscar nominee for movie *First Man*

What a fascinating story! The struggle with war, family, friends, life are amazing! It is both moving and inspirational. I am sure it will be a great success.

—Katherine Quinn
Author
Wife of the late Anthony Quinn

Captivating and gripping stories…so tactile it made me wants to reach for a scotch and soda and throw on a Sinatra CD.

—Bob Drury
Author of *The Rescue Season, Fatso, Mafia Cop, Mafia Cookbook, Incident at Howard Beach, Joe Dogs, The Life and Times of a Mobster, The Man with the Coke-Bottle Glasses*

An insider tactfully doesn't tell it all, but sure does let the reader in on the tormented life of a ten-year old child and later his flavor of the life around celebrities and heroes of this country.

—LeRoy Neiman
Artist

CHAPTER 1

Give a Little, Take a Little

The Greek mountain village of my birthplace Valtesiniko, nestled in a lush mountainside in the heart of Greece's southern region of Peloponnesus, was a far cry from the smoky nightclubs and glitzy celebrity hangouts of New York City. There were about three hundred little homes, maybe two stories high with white walls, wooden balconies, and red-tile roofs, blending into the greenery of the tall pine trees that carpeted the surrounding mountains. Those towering trees were the closest things we had to skyscrapers. I look back and remember them as these massive structures that stretched out forever into the clear azure sky. I've often thought that they seemed so much bigger to me because I was so much smaller then.

The only connection with the rest of the country was one narrow dirt road that snaked from our village through the mountains. It was rarely used, save for a rickety little truck that would come every two or three days to bring people and goods in and out of the village. It was the only reliable connection to the outside world, which was fine, as most of us saw little need to leave.

My father, Niko, ran a trading store from the street level of our house and would hitch rides on the truck for his trading trips to Tripoli, the commercial hub in our region a little more than fifty kilometers away. I can see myself, a scrawny seven-year-old, playing out in the dirt by our house with my siblings as the truck came clanking up the road, kicking up dust, carrying my father and a stash of mysterious goods from a faraway land.

He was a playful man, lanky, and always proud of his well-trimmed mustache. He sported a badge of patriotism in the form of a glass eye resulting from a war wound he'd received as a Greek soldier. When he'd see me, he'd pick me up and rub his mustache against my face, tickling my cheeks with the prickly hairs. I'd howl with laughter and pull at his mustache until my mother, Ifigeneia, came to rescue me. She was a beautiful young woman, always smiling and ready to make difficult times happier. In those early childhood years, there were many sweet moments, and I cherish them all.

Our village had an enviably simple message: give a little, take a little. We all took what we needed and gave what we could. The villagers were hardworking farmers with weather-beaten skin, bushy mustaches, and homemade sheepskin coats. Any outsider would look at them and see hardened, rugged, and gruff mountain people, but actually they were soft and kind, quick to laughter, and eager to help, and there was always a need for a helping hand. We were like one big extended family, and even in the toughest of times, we were happy.

But sometimes, the harsh winter months made life harder as they brought bitter cold and bouts of snowfall that made it difficult for anyone to accomplish anything, especially when so much of our world revolved around farming and outdoor life. My siblings and I spent those cold days by the fireplace, looking out at the mountains and trying to find joy in nature's beauty.

When the summer months came, all the villagers worked hard cultivating their plots, growing wheat, corn, and potatoes, and raising chickens and sheep to feed their families. But the people were more fertile than the fickle land, so each year their families grew larger and larger, forcing the elderly women of the village into midwife roles and making our resources scarcer.

Some of the villagers had very little, and others no money at all, so they traded goods for goods. They would drive their mules and donkeys to my father's store and trade eggs for soap, wheat for salt, milk for oil, or whatever it was that they needed. It wasn't Wall Street, but that's all they had.

Everything in our store came from Tripoli, and my father would return from his trips there with canvas bags filled with new merchandise, boots, clothing, salt, soap, and sugar. Meanwhile, my five siblings and I would hover nearby, stealing glances, anxious to see what new items he had brought this time. Even though we knew there was nothing for us, those moments had the excitement of Christmas morning.

There was no gas or electricity in our little village; a family was only as good as its strongest mule or donkey, which was the only means of machinery for power and transportation. Our donkey's name was Kitso. He was a large animal, bigger than the other donkeys in town, with bright brown fur and long ears, and he was a warrior. He did everything for us: carrying lumber, transporting bushels of wheat and corn, and hauling barrels of water from a faraway water fountain, along with all the firewood we needed for the winter.

We took good care of him and considered him a part of our family, and I believe he felt the same way. While everyone in our village shared animals to do their farming, Kitso stridently refused to take orders from anyone else. Instead, he would put his head down and walk in circles, kicking at any outsider who came near unless my father was present.

My father always had a strange connection with animals. Our cat, Cleri, was his shadow, always weaving between his legs as he walked, spending hours in the store during the work day, and sitting across his feet below the dinner table every night, believing that she was his protector.

Our village life centered on the many local churches that were scattered throughout town. Maybe it was the ubiquity of religion in our village that, as a boy, I always thought that I would become a priest. When I was a child, I don't think I ever imagined that; instead, I would eventually find myself in a luxurious supper club, somewhere in a concrete maze of tall buildings across the ocean, befriending the greatest icons of the era.

I would become friends with Yankees owner George Steinbrenner, make prank phone calls with the Yankee great Reggie Jackson, plan a movie with Anthony Quinn, and drive to Harlem with Frank Sinatra to share Christmas with the homeless. But for now, I was content with my idyllic mountain village life, my family, and the pine trees. The goods that circulated through my father's store offered us occasional glimpses into the rapidly changing world around us, but for most of us, that was more than enough.

There was one day when I got a real taste of the outside world that I'll never forget. I was playing on the hillside with my brother and sisters when I heard that old truck clanking up the dirt road toward our house, bringing my father back from his latest trip to Tripoli. The truck rolled up in the little square near our home, and as he began unloading his latest haul, we saw something that we had only heard about and seen in pictures or books. It was a shiny red-and-blue bicycle with a red rubber ball on the handlebars. As my father rolled it out of the truck, our eyes got wide, and our jaws hung ajar. For us children, the heroes of our Greek countryside, it was like seeing some sort of mythical creature, a Pegasus or a centaur, one that you only hear about in legend. My father squeezed the rubber ball, and it coughed out a crooked honk that made some neighbors lean out of their balconies, alarmed, to see.

As he walked the bicycle from the truck to our store, he was all business. He passed by us with a serious composure, and we stood there drooling. But his stoic attitude was disconcerting; he made us think he was bringing the bike into the store to be traded. There was a passing grief that only a child could grasp. He gave us a quick glance and continued walking the bike toward the store, honking its horn every couple of steps.

But then, just before he entered the store, he stopped, gave the horn a firm squeeze, and turned around with a playful grin, the kind of mischievous look he'd give me when he'd scratch my face with his mustache, a glint mysteriously appearing in his characteristic glass eye.

"What are you waiting for?" he asked. "Who gets the first ride?"

All of us rushed toward the bike in a panic. I don't remember who got there first. All I know was that, as the smallest, as always, I ended up on the ground. I looked up at my father and saw him standing there, laughing and reveling at the childish skirmish that he had ignited, and my mother came out of the house next to him, chuckling. To this day, I don't know what my father gave up getting that bicycle in Tripoli.

CHAPTER 2

Our Family

The story of our family, the Pavlopoulos family, is a story that spans two continents, blending a deep love of our homeland with a yearning for a land across the Atlantic. As a teenager, my father was a loyal Greek, but he was not like the rooted villagers that I had grown up with. He had adventure in his heart and a desire to search the world for a better life. He boarded a ship for America around 1916, where he embarked on a twentieth-century odyssey. He toiled in a Pittsburgh steel mill for four years and shared a room with other immigrants who all shared the same dream: to work hard and save their money until they could one day return home as rich men.

From the beginning, my father never planned on staying more than five or six years, but patriotism cut his plans short, and he voluntarily returned to Greece in 1920, along with a flood of loyal Greeks around the world, to defend the northern front of their country from a Turkish assault during the Albanian War. A Turkish bayonet struck his face and left him with a glass eye and scar for the rest of his life. Returning home to fight in the war was his patriotic duty to Greece, but it had left him with a faint sense of disillusionment, a distant belief that perhaps, one day, he would return to America, maybe this time with a family.

Even if my father didn't return to Greece a rich man as he had planned, he became a happy one after he asked his longtime flame, my mother, Ifigeneia, to be his wife. I remember her as a happy, energetic, and beautiful woman, whose round face always sported a big smile.

Our family was quite large; there were eight of us, including my parents. My oldest sister, Eleni, who grew up to be a nurse, was born first, then my brother, Pavlo, who would follow in my father's footsteps and become a merchant. My sister Kaiti was next, and she took my mother's route and became a housekeeper. But before I was born, my family faced a tragedy when their fourth child, Thalia, died at birth. The weight of that loss made my parents afraid of trying to grow their family for four years, lest they lose another child.

But in Valtesiniko, there were long, dark, cold winter nights with no TV, and sure enough, one day, I was born, healthy and strong, and that encouraged my parents to go back to work. Next were my younger sisters Marianthi and Fredericka. Fredericka got her name from a parliamentary rule that stipulated that the sixth child in every family, if a girl, would be baptized by a representative of the parliament and given the name of the Queen.

The six of us were a pack of troublemakers, yet despite the chaos that we undoubtedly caused my mother, she was always a positive woman, and that's what I remember most about her.

I remember her staying happy and positive, even when we left a little trail of destruction around our house. One of the consequences of not having much was that your own belongings, no matter how seemingly meager, felt invaluable. Something big, like our bike, was a luxury that many of us kids had imagined but had never seen in person. Before the bike, we had to make our own toys, and everyday things like my mother's knitting materials were always targets. I think, looking back, my siblings and I didn't quite grasp how much labor my mother put into those materials. The villagers would trade wool from their sheep in my father's store, and my mother would spend countless hours washing it and making string from it. When she wasn't looking, we would stow away with it, and we'd roll it into a makeshift ball and throw it around the house or in the dirt outside until it was torn and frayed and covered in mud. She would see it and scream, "Oh my God! Look at what you did!"

But her anger would always fade into a smile, and after a few moments, she would stop screaming and laugh about it. That's what she always did: she turned it into a teaching moment. In those experiences, getting yelled at after running around with the family's string, we learned how our world worked, that the little bit of string wasn't a ball in waiting; it was the sweater and socks we wore to keep warm. I can remember my mother reminding us of that fact, gently and with a big smile on her face.

However, the bike changed everything, turning my siblings and I into the focus of childhood wonder all over the village. My little sister Marianthi loved to hop on the handlebars and squeeze the horn relentlessly as I'd peddle us as fast as my toothpick legs could take us, flying through flocks of sheep. We'd cackle with laughter as they scattered, and the shepherds would throw their hands in the air behind us, screaming and cursing at us as we coasted off along the dirt roads. Our young friends Yannis and Costas would ask us for rides, and we would kindly oblige, acting like the generous monarchs of our world, a devilish bunch that ruled with the grace of King Paul and Queen Frederica. We were invincible.

When I look back on my childhood, though, I remember more than anything the villagers. They would tease and gossip, but to us, they were like aunts and uncles, brothers and sisters, and for better or worse, they were always there. My father's store was the nexus of life among the farmers in Valtesiniko, and I spent much of my time there, coming to know them all.

There was a fifteen-year-old loner named Leonidas who had somehow lost his family. I was too young to remember how, but my father pitied him and took him on as a helper around the store. There was also a little boy named Costas (whose stepfather often beat him) who would take shelter in our home, listening to my father as he taught us English words that he learned in America, which always invoked in me a strange curiosity that I couldn't yet describe. And I'll always remember a man named Mitso, a burly mountain farmer who, to me, looked like the biggest man on earth. He had a horse whose size was almost as impressive as his. When he came to the store, he'd lift me like I was a ragdoll and throw me up on top of the animal, taking me for rides around the village.

As I remember, it was a quiet, simple, and happy life. We were neither rich nor poor. But maybe, if my father had not had such a soft heart, he might have grown as rich as he had always hoped. He was always immensely sympathetic to the farmers and understanding of the extenuating circumstances that came with the unstable economy of agriculture.

If there was a bad draught, or if heavy rains destroyed the season's crops, farmers would have little to trade for essential goods to survive the harsh winters. He would give them whatever they needed on credit. Some appreciated his kindness, repaying however they could, often with manual labor. When he died, he left behind stacks of Bible-sized books, listing all of the outstanding credit that would go uncollected.

But there was one man who took advantage of his generosity. He was a guy in his thirties named Vassilis Kokkinis who had a cocky attitude, spending his time at the little tavern while others worked all day on their farms. Often, he would go to my father's store and take whatever he needed on credit. I can remember my mother saying to my father what we all already knew: "He's using you, Niko."

She warned that my father's kindness would only make Kokkinis lazier. Of course, my father knew that, but he also knew that Kokkinis had problems at home; his mother and his father were both sick and bedridden.

Spending time in my father's store, I could see that there was something different about him, and that the villagers always saw him as a patriarch of sorts. He was actually the elected mayor of Valtesiniko though that came with few official duties. I can remember a parade of people coming to our house and asking his advice on things such as the arranged marriages of sons and daughters, and he always tried to help them as best as he could.

I believe it was the time he spent in America that gave him his standing in the village as a knowledgeable leader. But even as the villagers respected him, they were wary of outsiders and seeped in nationalism, so his reputation as "the American" mystified many. His occasional English lessons were out of place to some. And as loyal as my father was to his homeland, he was entranced with American culture, which was foreign and odd for the people in the village.

For instance, the last Christmas before he died, he stunned the villagers by going out into the mountains with an ax all by himself. He returned dragging a small pine tree, and with little explanation, he stood it up in our house and started to adorn it with tiny balls of sheep wool, white as snow. It was a tradition he had learned in his travels, foreign in our homeland. As I think of it now, I'm sure it was Greece's very first Christmas tree.

Our neighbors who saw it were befuddled. "The American," they would say. "Look at him, dressing a tree. He's gone nuts." When I look back on that Christmas, I've often wondered if my father was preparing us for an eventual departure from Valtesiniko, for a new home in America that he'd never have the chance to offer us.

My father and mother, Niko & Ifigeneia Pavlopoulos

The house where I was born

As a young boy at 15

My village Valtesiniko, Arkadia, Greece

CHAPTER 3

When Our World Shifted

There was little reason for us to look beyond our idyllic lives in Valtesiniko. My biggest worries were the shepherds, shaking their fists at my sister and I as we sped through their flock of sheep on our bicycle. I was blissfully unaware that our world was shifting, approaching the brink of destruction.

In 1941, as my little sister and I chased sheep down the path on our bike, the seeds of World War II had taken root; Hitler was expanding his power, toppling nations like dominos and closing in on Greece. Looking back, I don't know if the people in my village were ever acutely aware of the threat, or if they were rather carrying on in harmony, paying little attention to the affairs of other worlds.

Hitler's army would finally arrive that year, and in the larger cities, like Athens and Tripoli, the impact was immediate. And soon, the Nazis' impact would reverberate out into the countryside. They forced the Greek government into exile, the king and queen fled to Egypt, and the absence of the monarchy left power vacuums across the country that eventually sent our villages into chaos.

That led to an underground movement of self-proclaimed "*antartes*," or rebels, who sought to fill the void of government, using the cover of patriotism as a rallying cry to gain power. In Valtesiniko, the ripples of war first arrived in the form of a small rebel group, camping out in the mountains, forging the beginnings of an uprising. They first approached my father, given his status as mayor, and invited him to meet with them in their camp.

As a nine-year-old child, I didn't know exactly what was going, but I remember one night, sometime later, when five armed strangers came into our house and spoke with my father in whispers. They were sitting at our kitchen table, and my mother offered them coffee as I sat by the fireplace, straining to hear their words.

Listening to their conversation, I could gather that my father had embraced them. His tone was friendly, and he offered them our house for whenever they needed a place to stay and our store as a source for supplies. I heard the armed men say that they had plenty of guns, supplied by England, but they needed fighters to join their cause. My father was excited. He saw these rebels as a brave group of young men, putting their lives on the line to stave off the invaders and restore our country. His adventurous spirit, the same one that carried him to America and sent him off to war in Greece, had been stirred again.

In hushed tones, he began spreading the good word of the rebels to our neighbors. "There is hope," he would tell them. "The liberators are coming." He told the villagers that they needed to support the rebels, and he encouraged them to join the cause. There was a steely determination in his face, a confidence and energy I had never seen before. I often wonder if this is what he was like in his youth in America, so self-assured and outspoken, unwilling to sit still and be swayed by the powerful. Or maybe it was his experiences there that had made him become that kind of man.

Not long after the first meeting with the rebels, the turmoil of the war began to hit our village hard. With Tripoli under Nazi rule, my father could no longer take his trading trips, and the store's shelves were increasingly barren. And privately, when my father wasn't talking about rebellions or urging our neighbors to action, I could see the worry in his face. He looked as if his whole life was a ball of string that my siblings and I had tossed in the dirt, and now his eyes skirted between each stray thread, trying to discern how he could possibly restore its shape. Soon, the rebels would become my father's greatest hope, and their scrappy sense of patriotism energized him.

With the store shelves empty, things got worse for the farmers, who could no longer trade their crops for goods. Things really fell apart when the unexpected happened: in August of 1941, there was a hailstorm with ice chunks as big as golf balls. They hit the farms and washed away the crops. I remember seeing all the villagers rush out to the fields in the aftermath, trying to sweep up and save what was left on the ground. But most of it was gone, only a few cornfields were saved, and hunger started to spread.

For the first time, my childhood happiness was shaken. We were hungry all the time, and the villagers even crushed up the corn-cobs at the mills to make tasteless flour for bread that filled up our bellies for a short while. There was no more happiness or laughter, no more bicycle rides through flocks of sheep. They had all been slaughtered, along with some cats and dogs, for food. Poverty, hunger, and fear quickly gripped us, coming as suddenly as the hailstorm that destroyed our livelihoods.

Eventually, in another world, the Allies landed in France and Italy, and the Germans started to withdraw forces from Greece to meet them in battle. The rebels began to take over the villages that the Germans left behind. They framed the German withdrawal as a retreat, providing a narrative of success that Greek villagers across the country began to cling to.

We were a hungry people in search of some heroes, and the perception of victory gave us our first taste of relief in years. None of us had ever truly understood the nuance of politics, and we'd never seen such complicated forces vying for power in our homes, and so we trusted the men who claimed to be our saviors. Soon, all of the villagers were feeling what my father had felt after his meeting with the rebels in our home: hope.

Their hope only grew as word spread about the rebels' supposed success. Their reputation as liberators became undisputed, and to support their claims, they began a robust campaign of guerilla war-fare against the stray factions of German forces who had been left behind to maintain Hitler's occupation. Perched out in the wilder-ness, the rebels would wait until Nazi troops passed by along nearby paths. They would emerge quickly, shoot and kill one or two soldiers, and then flee into the mountains.

Just the act of resistance alone was enough to energize our country. But we soon learned that there were consequences. The Germans enacted a cruel policy to counteract the rebels' outbursts, where, following an attack, the Germans would travel to the nearest town and kill ten of its residents for each German soldier killed. Then, they would burn the town to the ground, spreading scores of refugees out across Greece.

In Valtesiniko, that possibility gripped us with fear. Over the following months, the rebels continued to rest in our house and began spending more time there. For many, my father included, they seemed to be our only hope, even if their exploits had yielded only modest results. Nothing seemed more ruthless than the Nazi regime, and many in our village were prepared to risk everything to fight it. My father seemed more determined than ever.

I remember well the rebel leader, Christos Stasinopoulos; he was a man in his mid-thirties with a long and scraggly beard, bushy eyebrows, and cold eyes. He resembled the young Fidel Castro, always armed with an automatic machine gun and a pistol in his belt. He wore civilian's clothes and had a firm demeanor. With his followers, he kept a low profile, resting in our house for short periods before retreating to the mountains.

I was so young then, and I didn't understand everything, and maybe I don't remember everything exactly as it happened, or the complicated political storylines that helped create our situation, but as I listened to the grown-ups, and especially my father, I simply accepted that the rebels were seen as our heroes.

My family felt that we were pulling our weight for what we believed was the great patriotic cause of our time, and meanwhile, the rebels were recruiting volunteers from other villages in the region. From five or six, they grew to hundreds, and as the excitement persisted, I began to wish that I was old enough to join them. Eventually, around us, we started to feel a sense of urgency, all of us looking to the man with the scraggly beard to lead us from the brink of destruction.

CHAPTER 4

The Betrayals

One morning, I heard the church bells ringing faster than usual, not like they did for church, or in the mornings to start the school day. It was a startling sound; it caught the whole village's attention. A voice on a megaphone shouted, demanding that everyone, men and women, young and old, report to the town square where Stasinopoulos and his rebels were waiting.

On normal days in Valtesiniko, the bells of St. George's Church were the alarm clock on which our daily lives turned. It roused all of us children for school in the morning, clanging beside the church's stone walls.

Every two weeks, our teacher Vrahnos would designate someone from our class to go down to the church early in the morning and ring the bell to rouse all of the children in town for class. It was a thrill to be designated. You felt important; you felt that that each day only began with your permission, that the sun was roused only by your call. "Wake up now," those bells were saying. "The day has begun."

I remember the gravitas with which I accepted my responsibility. For two weeks, I held the power of our village in my hands, and I was anxious every day to get to the church and ring the bell. It was an adventure, and I would wake up earlier than everyone else, a harrowing 7:30 a.m. I'd quickly throw on whatever clothes I could find and run down to the church. I was terrified of being late and having to face the teacher.

The bell was on the side of the church, hanging from a tree. I was so small, always a small, thin kid, and the tongue inside the bell was heavy. You had to clang it against the sides of the round greenish dome as fast as you could. I remember, the first time, I thought it would be easy. I swung that tongue by the rope with all my might, and it just scraped against the brass side, leaking out a hollow, metallic scratch.

But on that morning, spurred on by the voice on the megaphone, it was the rebels who were ferociously ringing our church bells, and it sounded very different. They chimed with the rhythmic force of marching boots, jarring the villagers.

Everyone obeyed their orders and gathered in the little square. The rebels clogged up the streets, all holding automatic machine guns. We stood by, looking from side to side, wondering what was happening. Costas, my young friend, stood wide-eyed, close to his mother. The burly Mitso looked puzzled and intimidated, turning his head to others in the square to see if anyone could explain what was happening. Even the lazy Kokkinis was there, lurking off to the side, away from the rest of us.

I stood with my family, and my father stared forward with a scowl. He fixed his eyes on Stasinopoulos. It was a bit startling to see my father so fixated, and I wanted to call out to him, to ask him what was happening, but it seemed it would somehow be fruitless. The voice on the megaphone was still blaring, and those violent bells were still clanging. It wasn't like those days when us kids would sheepishly ring the bell to rouse the sun; at the hands of these burly men and their guns, even the sun would tremble. "Get up now," the bells seemed to say, "the revolution is beginning."

Finally, to capture everyone's attentions, Stasinopoulos fired a whole clip from his automatic machine gun up into the air. I can remember everyone in the square jolting backward with a gasp and then falling silent and intimidated. Still holding his machine gun high, he began speaking, making his first formal introduction to the people of our village. The villagers, hearing mostly rumors about the rebels from my father, surely did not expect such a forceful introduction.

I still can hear the sounds from that machine gun ringing in my ears and the chimes of our bells. Stasinopoulos stated with confidence that he and his men would liberate Greece from the Germans. And once the Nazis were gone, he said, the rebels would take over with a new regime, a communist regime. Communism—it was a word I had never heard before, but at its utterance, my father sighed. He was clearly caught by surprise, as was everyone else. Stasinopoulos raised his voice and spoke clearly so that the frightened faces in front of him would understand: "You will obey our rules. Those who oppose us will be killed."

It was like a frozen wind had passed through the square; everyone stood like a statue. Most of the villagers, especially us kids, did not understand what communism was. It was a word that was never spoken in our little mountain village. But at that moment, everybody was forced to understand that things had changed. There was a sense of panic and confusion as it became obvious that these were not the heroes my father had promised.

My father felt betrayed and was now facing the sinking revelation that he had let down his fellow villagers and his country. He gave Stasinopoulos a stern look and rushed into our house, shutting the door behind him. He didn't know it then, but that might have been the signature on his own death certificate. With my mother, we rushed to our house behind him and found him puffing profusely on his cigarette with eyes fixed on the floorboards.

Prior to Stasinopoulos's speech, my father had invited him and his closest followers to our house to eat and discuss their next steps. But as they filed into our house, my father was still despondent and puffing hard on another cigarette.

When these burly men with their automatic weapons walked into our house, I was frozen in confusion and fascination. It was the first time I had ever seen a weapon like that so close, and now, the air still seemed heavy with the shots that Stasinopoulos fired off in the square just moments earlier.

In my boyish mind, those machine guns made me feel curious, dumb, and helpless. It was an oddly similar feeling to when my siblings and I first saw our bicycle. Both the bike and the guns showed us a new realm of dreams from faraway lands. But if the bike brought dreams of sweetness and hope, those guns brought something dark and hazy, indiscernible but dreadful. If the bike was our Pegasus, then those guns were our Cerberus.

When everyone was seated, my father turned to Stasinopoulos, the corners of his mouth turned slightly downward into a stern frown. "Christo," he said, "this is not what we talked about."

He continued on to say that he had stuck his neck out to support a movement that would liberate our country, that he had vouched for these men, and talked of hope, democracy, and the restoration of Greece to its former greatness. He had never expected the intimidation, the threats, and this strange new word: communism.

"How am I going to face these people now?" my father asked.

Stasinopoulos just kept eating the chicken my mother had prepared. He never made direct eye contact with my father. "Things have changed, Niko," he said, very firmly and calmly. "That's how it's going to be."

My father got silent, and I've often wondered what he was thinking in those moments. He was a loyal Greek, and I saw on his face a sense of shame, a belief that he had brought some illness to his home country and let down the people who put their lives in his hands. He realized now that Stasinopoulos was not the patriot he presented himself to be. Rather, he was an enemy of the country that my father loved so much. And with the Nazis still keeping their hold on Greece, it was clear that there was no lesser of two evils. There was only evil.

When the rebels left, the friendly demeanor that they once had with our family was no longer there, and there were no handshakes, no pleasantries. That was the first time that I saw my mother's face without its glow. It lacked the beautiful smile that could turn all pain into happiness. She was scared and gloomy. Later that night, I could overhear her warn my father in a low and shaking voice that he should watch his words carefully. The rebels would not tolerate resistance.

"I feel sorry for our country," he whispered back. "They will start a civil war."

As a nine-year-old boy, I didn't quite understand what was happening. I could feel the clouds hanging over our town, but I clung to a childlike faith in my parents, knowing that as long as they were around, our life would prevail.

In the meantime, hundreds of uneducated farmers from villages across the country were misled and continued their adoration for the rebels. It was the fruit of the rebels' deadly propaganda campaign. They went on with their wartime exploits, killing one or two Germans at a time, and returning to the people preaching victory. And when the Germans would kill ten villagers and burn down whole towns, the rebels would return, feeding on grief and fear, promising to bring an end to the bloodshed.

The farmers took up arms and were prepared to die for Greece, not fully understanding the horrors that a communist regime could bring. In our village, men like Kokkinis, the lazy farmer, felt that they had finally found their worth. He became a confidant for Stasinopoulos, lurking about town to keep a watchful eye on our people, to ensure that everybody stayed loyal. He said little, but his presence spoke volumes. To see Kokkinis around was like seeing the scraggly beard of Stasinopoulos himself.

Some villagers were quick to come to my father's store to talk to him, demand answers, and discuss the next steps. They knew how dangerous it was to gather and have such talks. They spoke in whispers and were always careful to avoid being in earshot of rebel loyalists like Kokkinis. I suppose it would have been easy for them to be angry with my father. He was, after all, the mayor of our town, and he had vouched for these strange new men and given them passage into our lives. But as I have said, our village was a family, and those who were willing to take the risk understood that we were stronger together. Quietly, the cauldron of resistance began to bubble within our house's walls.

There was no doubt, however, that our village had been shaken. In those days, I heard that word "communism" many times. Like many of the villagers, I was confused by it. It was a word that people seemed very afraid of, like it was some folkloric spirit haunting the mountains, the type of thing that you needed to knock on wood three times or draw a line of salt to keep it away. I didn't pay much mind to the word, but it was clear that it had brought a shadow into our lives.

The communists had inserted a fear into our lives, and even as the villagers tried to work together, they were forced to do so secretly. People passed by one another on the street, hardly lifting their eyes. All conversations happened in hush voices in quiet corners, and few dared to speak of current events. Communists frequently came through our town wielding weapons. But they didn't need guns to scare us; just as frightening was the possibility that one of their men could be listening.

I'm not sure if my siblings ever had a clearer idea of what was going on. But I knew my father did, and one night, as he sat in his chair near the fire, I decided to ask him what communism was, and he looked surprised to hear that word come from the mouth of his young child. I could see in his eyes a brief moment of thought, but he didn't answer me directly; instead, he told me something that made me wonder. It was a message of a future that I would one day know better. It was the first time he had ever spoken so openly to me about his journey.

"When I was a young man, I traveled to America," he said. "The people are free to believe in anything they want, without being afraid of being killed by those who don't believe the same thing. It's a wonderful place."

He was very positive, happy even.

"Maybe someday, we'll all go there," he said.

I didn't yet understand why he was telling me this, but there was such sweet relief in his voice and a childlike twinkle in his glass eye. It reminded me of the warm summers, riding our bicycle through flocks of sheep. But my mother became concerned hearing him speak of such dreams.

We were all very aware of my father's reputation in town as "the American," a label that, for some, made him different. And in the highly divisive and politicized atmosphere that the communists had created, it was feared that the mere mention of a foreign entity like America could give the communists cause to question his motivations. It would not take long for them to discover the discontent brewing in our household and among our neighbors.

My mother was acutely aware of that, and when she heard him talking to me so wistfully, she stopped him.

"This is not the time for such talk," she said, tears swelling in the back of her throat. I didn't think it was possible to see such fear inside my family's home.

"Don't talk about it again," she said. "They will kill you."

It was a blunt reality that I had never even known was possible.

My father got silent. He only pointed up to a handmade embroidery inscription hanging on the wall behind him with the Greek words: "To Pepromenon Fygin Adynaton."

In English: "It's Impossible to Avoid what is Destined."

I still have that embroidery. My daughter, Effie, found it on her visit to Valtesiniko many years later. She brought it to me, and it hangs in my dining room in Jackson Heights, Queens.

My father never made it back to America. I've often thought that, had he lived, he would have moved us all there, a country that never stopped tugging at his heart. But I would always remember the way he described it to me that day. He planted the idea of America and its promise of freedom deep inside my chest. And one day, it would tug at my heart too.

It's Impossible to Avoid what is Destined

CHAPTER 5

Shattered

On the evening of April 30, 1944, my father came up from the store to sit at the table with us for dinner, and, as always, our cat Cleri followed him, weaving in and out between his legs before taking her usual spot at his feet beneath the table. We talked, laughed, and got scolded a little for our misbehaviors. My mother had somehow acquired the ingredients to make yogurt, which we had not had since before the war started. When she laid it out onto the table, it triggered a contest between my siblings and I as we raced to see who could get the first dollops of the creamy delicacy.

There were these moments, sometimes, when things felt simple again. That's all they were, moments, but this one was particularly sweet. It was just the sense of regularity, that for the first time in months, life seemed to be normal.

However, there was a cloud above us that we couldn't see. Cleri, who had been sitting peacefully at my father's feet, seemed to be struck by something supernatural. She let out a high-pitched screech, jumped out from beneath the table, and started flailing her claws wildly. She nicked my father on his cheek, and he yelped and jumped out of his chair. She kept flailing, bouncing up and down off the top of the table like a rubber ball, sending dishes flying through the air and flinging the bowl of yogurt across the room.

My mother, fearing that Cleri had rabies or some other disease, grabbed a broom and chased her out onto the balcony, but the cat kept screaming, jumping, and scratching the door, eager to get in and continue her attack. Cleri had never behaved like this before, and the outburst made us all anxious. All of us pitched in and cleaned up everything in silence, and we went to bed uneasy, still listening to the cat's screams. In those days, even the slightest disturbance felt significant, like strange forces reminding us that we were no longer the authors of our own story.

On the following morning of May 1, as dawn slowly began to break, Cleri's screams had stopped, but we were all stirred awake by the sound of barking dogs and rumbling footsteps coming up the stairs to our second-story house. Before I could shake the sleep from my eyes, there was a crack as Stasinopoulos and three of his communists knocked down the front door and stormed in, yelling with guns drawn. Sporting long, greasy beards, and raggedy clothes, they looked like biblical demons, and their yells were deafening.

We all rushed behind our parents, scared and shaken, but seeing Stasinopoulos there, we felt somewhat relieved. After all, we all knew him well, fed his followers, and quartered them in our home like they were family. The only thing that registered in my mind was that this was some kind of misunderstanding and that everything would be all right until I heard my father asking, "Christo, what are you doing? What do you want?"

Stasinopoulos kept his stern expression. "Outside for some questions," he demanded.

My father, still in his long johns, turned to his room to put on pants. But he was grabbed by two of the communists and dragged outside.

We knew then that any questions that they had were already answered. Screaming, we all rushed after them. One communist caught my mother and kept her in the house as we ran outside. They were marching my father down the road to a neighbor's house, and I could hear desperation in his voice. He knew what was happening.

"Christo, think of my children...think of my children..." he pleaded.

Those were my father's last words.

But there was no response. The man who my father once saw as the liberator of our country, now had his gun ready, forcing my father to walk in front of him wearing only his long johns. Others pointed their guns on us, threatening to shoot if we got any closer as Stasinopoulos ordered my father to stop in front of our neighbor's house.

As I grew older, I would watch movies where the hero died, and in his last breaths, he would deliver a stirring monologue. Maybe he'd tell his family that he loved them. Maybe he'd stall the villain long enough for a deus ex machina. Or maybe all he'd have time for is a wistful "goodbye." But real tragedies aren't so forgiving. Life falls from the body swiftly, like water dumped from a glass. My father didn't even have time to turn around and look at us one last time.

In one movement, Stasinopoulos pointed the gun behind my father's head and pulled the trigger. We all jumped at the crack. There was a thud as his body hit the ground and a pool of blood oozed from underneath his head.

That moment played out so quickly, and part of me believed I was still asleep, that this was just a bad dream, but I could see their faces and my father's lifeless body on the ground. I heard my mother and my siblings scream. I felt sickness in my stomach, and I wanted to vomit. My mouth tasted like blood.

My eyes were fixed on Stasinopoulos as he walked by and gave me a stern look. He didn't know it yet, but this ten-year-old would grow up fast. He walked into our neighbor's house, where our friend Kapelianis had been lying sick in his bed for weeks, and one shot rang out followed by a woman's and a little boy's screams. I knew then that my schoolmate George had also lost his father.

We were crying and screaming at the communists who then turned their guns on us and forced us back into our house. There, we found more communists ransacking the place and taking everything. Others, meanwhile, emptied out whatever was left in my father's store.

Meanwhile, many other rebels went from house to house and gathered all the villagers, including the women and children, and brought them to the edge of the village in a place called Rahi where Stasinopoulos was holding a paper containing a list of names. He called out the names of fifteen villagers, and they stepped out in front of him. He ordered his followers to tie their hands and march them away while their families cried hysterically, knowing they would never see them again. As we learned later, all fifteen were marched into the mountains, where they were tortured and thrown off of a cliff to meet a horrible death.

Earlier that morning, Stasinopoulos and his confidant Kokkinis were seen together, and rumors surfaced that Kokkinis was the author of the death list, and later, one of his cousins verified that the rumors were true.

There were many reasons that my father became a target. It could have been his time in America, his playful reputation as "the American." Perhaps that had sparked some fear and questions about his loyalty. Or maybe he was simply overheard talking to the villagers about his concerns. Or maybe the frequent visitors to his store and hushed conversations didn't go unnoticed. But my mother believed, until she died, that Kokkinis put my father's name on the death list because of the massive debt he had accumulated at my father's store, the pages and pages of credit we all knew would never be paid.

I wasn't there in Rahi as Stasinopoulos read out the death list. We were kept in our house the whole time, with the rebels training their guns on our faces, and when they finally left, I looked out the door and saw four villagers had put my father's body on a blanket and were carrying him toward the house.

Everything around me became dark and hazy. My siblings cried, but their screams seemed to come from some faraway place. In my childish stupor, or maybe in some form of wishful thinking, I convinced myself that he had somehow survived the bullet, that he was alive. A flash of thoughts raced through my mind: he had survived war before, I thought. He had survived a bayonet to the eye, for God's sake. Surely this would be no different; surely, he would survive again. As my siblings cried, my eyes remained dry, and I tried to be a good brother and comfort them, telling them that he could still be alive. My older sisters, meanwhile, tried to find the words to tell me I was wrong. My mother, weeping, took us all into the kitchen, closed the door, and waited there. None of us knew what would happen next.

Finally, a family friend who we called Aunt Fotena came in the kitchen and asked my mother for my father's clothes and shoes.

He had to be alive! I thought. *Why else would they need his clothes and shoes?*

But then, as my wishful thinking grew stronger, I heard a hammering outside in our yard. I looked out and saw Antoni, our village carpenter, making a coffin. And that's when I started to cry. As I stood there watching Antoni finishing the coffin, my hopes faded away and reality sank in, and I knew my father was dead.

Later, Aunt Fotena came back and took us all back to the room where my father was lying dead in his coffin. I was crying when I knelt down next to him, and I looked at the scarring around his missing left eye, the price he paid for protecting his country.

But then I looked at the hole in his nose from where the bullet had exited, fired by Stasinopoulos. I thought about how my father fought for this country and its entire people, including Stasinopoulos. When I looked at that wound, I remember feeling like a different person. My face got hot, and my insides turned, like there was something, a scream or a force, growing so quickly it would burst through my skin to get out.

I stopped crying, and I never wanted to cry again. From that moment on, I was no longer a child. I had become a raging young man crammed inside a scrawny child's body that had only one thought: kill both Kokkinis and Stasinopoulos. I silently promised my father that I would do that. From that moment, I became an angry vigilante kid.

CHAPTER 6

The Aftermath

In villages like ours, there was a tradition at funerals where women would come dressed in black from head to toe as professional mourners, wailing and singing songs of death. They knelt around my father's coffin, weeping and singing all night, leading everyone in prayer and tears. The next morning, a priest came and said a prayer before we held a procession and lowered him into his grave.

I'm sure my father, the mayor of our town, would have been disappointed. Very few villagers showed up; they were all afraid of becoming targets. Mourning for "the American" was a danger that few would risk. It was a sad irony that the man who they turned to for everything would be laid to rest in front of so few.

When I think back on it now, I remember that Cleri, our cat, had been one of the few who remained loyal to my father until the end. She had been out all night, screeching and howling until the dawn. It's believed that cats and other animals can foresee danger. Perhaps she was trying to warn him. Or perhaps she was hosting her own funeral that night, singing into the dawn, trying to rouse the neighbors to join and mourn for a death that only she knew would happen. Nonetheless, after my father was killed, she never came home again and was nowhere to be found.

Everything came crumbling down after that. The rebels were getting stronger and spread fear like fire. Nobody trusted one another anymore, and in fact, nobody spoke. Valtesiniko had become a dystopia of fear and sorrow; even the church bells lost their magic.

I recall an incident that threatened the entire village. One day, the Germans were passing through our village, a difficult task given the mountainous terrain. Beyond our village, it was very difficult for travelers to use automobiles, and so the Germans stopped to gather all of the villagers' donkeys and mules so they could load up all their equipment and pass through the mountains.

Two young German soldiers arrived at our home and noticed our family donkey, Kitso. We were terrified; we knew that Kitso would never cooperate with strangers. All of us stood on our balcony and watched with uneasy breath as the German soldiers tried to wrangle Kitso. They pulled at his reins, but Kitso pulled back. He stuck his head down, walked in agitated circles, and kicked up dust behind him. The Germans grew impatient, and one of them approached a pile of firewood, grabbed a large branch, started to beat Kitso into submission.

But Kitso was a stubborn animal that, like my father, was unwilling to yield to intimidation. Before the German took his third swing, Kitso flailed his legs in the air and connected with the man's jaw and chest. The soldier fell to the ground with a thud, and his companion rushed over to him, but it was too late. His comrade was already dead. I remember feeling sick to my stomach. Even then as a child, I knew what was at stake. I, too, had heard the stories of the scorched villages and understood the cloud of death that these German soldiers brought with them. All I could do was pray that my family would not be killed, that our neighbors would not be killed, that our homes, our churches, our schools, would not be scorched.

As we watched that German boy's body, limp on the ground, all we felt was fear. We could feel life itself hanging, paused. In my mind, I ached to hear those rickety tires of the truck, to see my father smiling with his glass eye, unloading his haul of goods from Tripoli. Those memories seemed so fragile then, like my whole life was an insignificant piece in a game played by hateful, foolish men.

I suppose the Germans realized that it was the animal that caused the soldier's death, and not anyone in our village, and thankfully, they spared us. A troop of men walked over to the soldier's lifeless body and, without a word, picked him up and buried him at the edge of town as we waited breathlessly. But they left Kitso, took what animals they could, and headed off into the mountains without saying a word to us. And while he may have never understood his fortunes, Kitso was the only donkey that evaded Valtesiniko's German animal draft.

In our house, after my father's death, the immediate aftermath was desolate. The rebels took everything and left us with nothing: no clothes, no food, no store, and no father to provide for us, to take the trips in the rickety truck to Tripoli. It was just the four walls around us, and no one dared to give us any help.

They all feared that Kokkinis or someone else would see them and make another death list. When I read the news today and hear about the atrocities committed by ISIS, or other terrorists around the world, I see my family, to a certain extent. I see the same fear in those victims, and I see the same hate and violence surrounding them.

There were only two people who risked everything to help us in the days that followed. Aunt Fotena, like us, had nothing, but she came to us when no one else would, to bring us some food and comfort in a time when our family was grieving. She would come over and talk with my mother, helping us salvage a sense of normalcy. I don't know if she wasn't afraid, or if she felt that as a woman she would be safe, or if she simply didn't understand the risks, but nevertheless, she would survive the atrocities of the rebels and has always held a special place in my memories.

My father's cousin, Uncle Vassili, also helped us to survive. He was a rabbit hunter and very close with my father. At night, he took a great risk by walking past our house and throwing bread and food through the window, before skulking away under the cover of darkness.

But really, our biggest hero was my mother. As I've said, she was always a positive woman. Throughout my childhood, I never heard her complain, and aside from that nightmarish morning on May 1, she never cried again. I suppose there were times when she found herself alone; she may have released the burdens that she carried. But in front of us, her six children, she was a rock, the one who kept our little machine moving.

To feed us, she did what she always did: rolled up her sleeves and got to work. She taught us how to cultivate the garden to grow potatoes and vegetables, working hard on her hands and knees to grow our food. She started raising chickens by herself, and as the grieving slowly subsided, we saw glimmers of her positivity, her glowing smile that once warmed our home. If we ever complained about work, my mother would tell us, "Complaining won't fill your bellies. Keep working and God will look after us."

After the Germans left Greece, my mother somehow got my older sister, Eleni, out of Valtesiniko and into a nursing school in Athens. My brother, Pavlo, eventually made an effort to reopen our father's store, but it was quickly apparent that the villagers were too scared to come. He went off to Tripoli to work as we kept things going the best we could.

And so, we kept on surviving, doing our best to keep our world running. But my anger never went away. My little ten-year-old mind had been furiously spinning, searching for a way to find and kill Stasinopoulos and Kokkinis, and to fulfill the promise I made to my father. But being alone and helpless, all I ever got was frustration and anger. I remember that every day, I'd go to my aunt's vacant house at the edge of the village and break into her empty stable. There, amid the garbage and debris, I'd find a pair of empty cans that had been left behind, and I'd fantasize that I'd found the two men that I'd been looking for. I'd beat those cans mercifully for what felt like hours, screaming and cursing them, letting my anger loose. But the anger never dissipated. The next day, I would go back again and start another beating. I suspect that my search for revenge had driven me close to the edge of insanity.

One day, desperate to complete my mission, I stole my mother's kitchen knife and spent days secretly sharpening it against a rock, and practicing in my father's empty store when no one was around. The knife was very flimsy, and I started to worry that my attempts might fail since I was so small. I knew then that I would need something stronger, perhaps a gun like the ones that the communists fired off in our village square. I became determined to find one, knowing that my mission depended on it.

CHAPTER 7

Human Shields

Months after my father's death, the Germans were all but gone from Greece, but that did little to mitigate the communists' stranglehold on our lives. Other villages had started to mount a resistance against them, refusing to accept their communist regime. These larger towns, with more people, had heard about the atrocities committed in villages like ours, and they decided to make a stand.

But with the opposition came only more tragedy, as Greece descended into civil war and families continued to be torn apart. To bring these towns into submission, the communists developed a horrific new strategy to assert their power called Pedomazoma. They kidnapped hundreds of kids from ages ten to fifteen and marched them on the front lines of their battles, turning them into unwitting human shields that would cripple entire armies whose men wouldn't fire upon kids.

One day, those church bells started ferociously ringing again. We heard a familiar husky voice over a frazzled megaphone ordering everyone to gather in the square. We didn't know what was waiting for us there, but we knew it was bad.

It was a warm September afternoon, but the bells chilled our spines. When we had all gathered, we stood silently, staring at the armed communists, waiting to see what they wanted this time, or what would happen. Suddenly, without uttering a word, the communists descended upon the crowd, picking out the strongest looking boys and girls, tearing them away from their families and bringing them to the other side of the square. Mothers and fathers screamed and clutched their children. The rebels used their rifle butts to strike out at anyone who tried to resist, hurling threats of death as they did so.

I looked into the crowd and could see bloodied desperate faces. The rebels' faces, by contrast, were cold, like they were cattle farmers, picking out young animals for slaughter. Many of the children cried, reaching out to their parents. Others seemed still, as if even in their young age, they possessed the unfortunate wisdom that life was always short and cruel.

As a communist rebel approached my sisters and me, I can remember seeing my mother tug nervously at her hair. Without a word, he grabbed me and began dragging me over to another part of the square where four other children waited nervously. My mother sprang into action, screaming and beating at his back until he turned around and pointed his gun to her face.

At that moment, I felt a terrible pain. I recalled a tragic episode that much of our village had witnessed the summer before, where a young mother who was working at her farm hung a basket carrying her newborn child from a tree branch. She believed that her child was safe from snakes and other wild animals on the ground, only to see an eagle swoop down, grab the child from its blankets, and fly off. I imagined this young mother as she reached out into the sky, desperate, screaming. I could see my mother bearing the same face, as the rebel walked away with me, with not a thing in the world she could do.

No one knew then why the rebels were amassing children. We eventually learned that it was all part of their cowardly agenda to use us as human shields.

In that moment, I believed I would die. I can remember looking back at my mother as she stood with terror in her eyes, grabbing her hair in fistfuls. I wasn't sure if she could handle another loss, and I hoped that she and my sisters would survive.

At ten years old, I had accepted death. But it wasn't all that surprising. We had lived in fear for so long, and the only life we could remember was one of war, fear, and hunger.

They took six of us, and along with eight children they had taken from other towns, they marched us like sheep toward another town called Magouliana about ten kilometers away that was protected by an anti-communist group of townspeople who had begun to fight back. The rebels just marched behind us, cold, with their guns ready.

When we came closer, I could see guards in their bunkers stirring to take their positions, apparently having noticed us. I was terrified that they might shoot on sight, before realizing that it was children who marched toward them. All I could do was pray that they would see us before they fired. The thought of running away quickly disappeared, for behind us, the communists stood ready to shoot at the slightest sign of insubordination. With each step I was expecting death, but even in these terrifying moments, the thought of failing to keep my promise of vengeance to my father was all-consuming. I felt that the story I had written for myself, where I was the hero fighting for justice, would never come true.

As children, we tend to think in stories. We make templates from the tales that our parents tell us in the warmth of our homes. The good guy always wins, and the bad guy always loses. I had seen too much in my short life to believe that was true. But even still, I believed in my gut that suffering was rewarded with vindication.

Walking across that field, trying to control my breathing and stumbling with every step, I feared that vindication would never come, and more than anything else, I felt disappointed that I would never have my chance.

I wouldn't die that day, thank God. The men defending the town had seen us and realized what was happening, and rather than take part in a massacre of children, they allowed the communists to take over the town without a fight, and the rebels, for some reason, allowed us to return back to our homes.

After that, those bells in our town never sounded the same to me again. Every time I heard them, I'd run and hide somewhere. I remember one time, when they started to ring, I ran to a rundown home that had been abandoned for many years. In the weeds out in the backyard, there was an old brick oven. I thought it was the perfect place to hide, and when I tried to crawl in, I felt something in the back that wouldn't let me fit my small body all the way in. When I pulled it out, I discovered it was a bag with old clothes wrapped around a small machine gun with two full magazines. My eyes were drawn to the gun; it was like the one Stasinopoulos fired off that day in the square. As I looked at it, I could still hear the loud roar of its bullets, could still feel the power hanging in the air. I knew then I had found the partner that I had been looking for, the partner that would help me get the revenge that I so desperately wanted. I picked it up with both hands like it was a Christmas present. It was heavy and metallic, cold to the touch, but to me, it was like picking up something gold.

At that moment, I felt that I had found an angel to help me carry out my mission. I felt powerful again, like the king of my kingdom, like the kid with the cool bicycle that everyone wanted to try.

I was invincible. I didn't care or think about the possibility that this gun might turn me into a killer. That thought never crossed my mind. I stayed there for a long time, and I started making my plans. When it became dark enough, I took my newly found friend to my father's now empty store and hid it in between the walls.

The only person I told about the gun was my sister Kaiti. With my older sister, Eleni, in school, my older brother, Pavlo, in Tripoli and my two sisters Marianthi and Fredericka too young to understand, Kaiti and I had an especially close relationship.

Every day, I would spend hours at the store practicing how to use the gun; pulling out the clip and pulling the trigger to hear the click was a thrill. For the first time, I had that sense of childish joy back into my life. It was an automatic machine gun that I planned to use to kill my father's killers.

CHAPTER 8

A Taste of Revenge

I hear people say, forget about, let it go, it's in the past. But some things just don't go away because you want them to.

The Allies eventually landed in Greece and swept through the country. When word spread that they were coming to our region in Peloponnesus, the communist rebels went into a panic and scattered into the mountains to hide. While others in our village felt happy and free, I was subdued. I began to think of Stasinopoulos and Kokkinis, hiding somewhere in the mountains, alive and well. I had to find them.

One day, I took my machine gun and went up to the mountains and hid behind some thick bushes near the mouths of some of the caves where I suspected rebels were hiding out. I could see them moving along the hillside, entering and exiting the mountains' cave networks. I was no more than fifteen feet away from them, and I clung tight to my gun, ready to fire if I saw Stasinopoulos or Kokkinis. I knew I could have killed them all with one burst but only wanted the two I was looking for.

Every day, I returned to that same spot and waited there, scanning the faces of those defeated, lethargic men, hoping to see my targets. I felt like a bloodhound, trying to get a trace of their scent, always ready to pull the trigger. But with each passing day, my hopes started to slowly fade.

One day, the Greek fighters who had joined the Allies finally arrived in Valtesiniko, cheered and welcomed by all of us. We all rushed out into the streets to thank them with our hands clasped together in signs of prayer and gratitude. These men were the true liberators that we had always hoped for. They helped us feel safe again. The people in our village began to talk to one another again without the fear of being put on Kokkinis's death list.

When I first saw those soldiers, I began to idolize them, wishing that I could one day join them. I followed them around everywhere and eventually, I volunteered myself as a guide through the mountains to the caves where I knew I had seen the rebels hiding. They trusted me, and to my joy, allowed me to carry my gun. Little did I know that one day in America, I would become one of them, embarking on a journey that would eventually lead to me befriending the greatest war hero of all time: Audie Murphy.

I would help the soldiers navigate the rugged terrain and show them where the neighboring villages were. I'd point out the caves, and the soldiers would fire a barrage of mortars, flushing out groups of rebels like ants from an anthill, with hands in the air, surrendering.

Like a hawk in the sky, I'd squint and scan their faces, clinging to my gun and searching for Kokkinis and Stasinopoulos. I never let the soldiers know about my plan of killing them, and I never decided if I would shoot them on sight or if I would say anything to them first. That wasn't important to me; all I wanted was to find them and kill them. But as each day passed, I began to fear they had slipped away.

All the captured communist rebels had to be sent by trucks to Tripoli for trial in the local court system. But everybody knew that those were kangaroo civilian courts, with many judges who were relatives or acquaintances to the communists. Many of the rebels were released, enraging villagers and the families of victims. The soldiers understood and grew angry as well, but there was nothing that they could do; they had their orders. I was desperate to find Stasinopoulos and Kokkinis before they were captured and sent to those Kangaroo courts and set free, and so tagging along with the soldiers was my only hope.

One day, I was home waiting for our next trip to the mountains and I heard a big commotion coming from the little square of the village, so I rushed to see what was happening. As it turned out, another group of soldiers returned to Valtesiniko from a different part of the mountains with a prisoner. They had him on a Jeep, guided by four soldiers ready to take him to Tripoli. But some villagers recognized him. It was Kokkinis, the man who'd authored the death list that resulted in the murders of our beloved seventeen villagers. The people rushed the Jeep in an attempt to stop it from leaving.

Their screams were heard all over the village, and it didn't take long for everyone to rush to the square, demanding that Kokkinis be turned over to them. By the time I got there, the situation had escalated into a riot.

I knew now that the man I was looking for was right there, just a few feet away and I had to get to him first. But my small and skinny posture made it difficult for me to push my way through that angry crowd. I crawled between legs and feet. I was kicked and stepped on and finally reached the Jeep. I climbed on it, and as soon as I saw Kokkinis, I reacted like a possessed and uncontrollable animal. I clawed at his throat, thinking only of killing until one soldier grabbed me and struggled to pull me away.

Finally, I was separated, thrown from the Jeep like a pillow, but I took joy in the fact that I'd managed to sink my fingers into Kokkinis's throat and nicked him. While I was on the ground, I looked down and saw his blood on my fingers.

I know how it must sound, an eleven-year-old, so intent on killing, but this man had betrayed my father's kindness and dismantled my life. If I had changed into something shameful, a violent, rage-driven young man haunted by anger, it was Kokkinis who had changed me. I wondered how my father would have reacted. Would he have been so kind to him then, shown him the same patience and compassion as he did in his store, knowing this man marked him to be killed? I don't know the answer to that. I don't know if I'd have reacted differently now. But in that moment, I was happy, and I instantly wanted more.

I think it still feels good now, to think of it. I don't think anyone can understand that feeling unless they've experienced that level of loss. Loss rewires your brain and unleashes an anger that grips your heart and stirs you as if it were an ordinance from God Himself, a voice calling on you to right the wrongs and restore the balance of good and evil. Some days you want to scream at Him for putting such an unbearable weight on your shoulders. But to feel so close to fulfilling that calling, to see the blood on your fingertips, it's intoxicating.

Our square had descended into chaos, and more soldiers had come to try and clear a path for the Jeep, and I feared that the villagers would soon be defeated, allowing my one chance to get Kokkinis to slip away. So in desperation, I ran back to my house and grabbed my machine gun, and I had to act fast.

The road that leaves from Valtesiniko to Tripoli goes through the mountains, with sharp curves and hardly enough space for two automobiles to pass each other. I knew a shortcut that led through the mountains and to a part of the road on the outskirts of town. I had learned it from my days of romping around the countryside as a free child, roaming with packs of other free children, getting into the mischief that children seek. I began climbing up the mountainside, feeling as if I were again a free child.

I reached a particularly sharp curve of the road that brought me out of view from the village. I began stumbling up and down the mountainside, rolling down big rocks, and stacking stones from the side of the road to create a barrier, anything that would stop that Jeep from passing through.

When I had a modest pile, I ducked behind it with my machine gun and waited. My heart was pounding so hard; I thought maybe it was the sound of boots walking along the path, but I kept my mind focused on the road, peeking from behind the rocks to see if the Jeep would appear from behind the bend.

Finally, I heard the Jeep's engine chugging up the road, and as it came around the curve, I heard its tires creak to a halt. I saw two soldiers jumping out with guns drawn, advancing toward me behind the pile of rocks while two others stayed in the Jeep to guard Kokkinis. Before they could get too close, I stepped out with my gun pointed at the Jeep. I thought back to my march on Magouliana, and how the guards would rather flee their positions than fire upon children and felt a little confident that these soldiers wouldn't hurt me. And if they did, so be it. I truly didn't care whether I lived or died.

"He is mine, and I am willing to die," I yelled out to them.

The soldiers were clearly surprised, seeing an eleven-year-old with a machine gun. But they remained calm. One of them seemed to be the ranking officer, and witnessing my emotions, he ordered Kokkinis to get out of the Jeep.

When Kokkinis stumbled out, he looked nothing like how I had inflated him to be in my imaginations of this moment. I expected a bold and evil man. Instead, what stood before me was a hunched and trembling thing, likely malnourished from weeks in the mountains. I didn't pity him. My gun clattered in my hand as a nervous energy flowed through my body, and I begged it would never stop. I liked watching him sweat, felt manic as I held his life before me like it were an insect's.

"I am the son of Niko Pavlopoulos," I told him.

He flinched at my family name; I saw a flash of recognition in his eye, a sense of panic on his face. I loved that feeling, seeing him fear me, and I stared at him longer. I thought of standing over my father's body, looking at his missing eye. It was because of Kokkinis that everything ended the joy of riding our little white and blue bike and chasing sheep.

I embraced what he had made me. I won't lie. I enjoyed it. I wanted this moment to last forever, where I could watch the realization in his eyes that this was his last day on earth. *I would pull this trigger, and I would be at peace,* I thought. I would be able to be happy again, to wake each morning without feeling the bells' cacophonous reverberations in my head and the call to violence in my heart. All I'd have to do was pull the trigger. I felt my finger touching the trigger, ready to pull it and let bullets rip through Kokkinis's body; it was something that I wanted to do since the day my father died. I had reached my moment.

Suddenly I heard a gunshot, and Kokkinis's body clumped to the ground. I knew I hadn't fired my gun, and I looked over and saw the ranking officer holding his pistol toward my demon. I looked at him, and his gaze turned at me. I felt a heat rise from my waist to my throat, and something snapped in that moment. I felt that I was cheated, robbed of something that I had longed for so deeply and had hunted for so long. Years of imaginations and daydreams, planning and scheming, hiding in the walls of my dead father's store with a gun that had fatefully fallen into my fragile hands, all of it for nothing. Inside, there was a deep and hollow feeling that I had failed my father, that his killer would not know the justice that he deserved came from me.

My gun shifted to the officer; I was no longer in control of my actions. I screamed with all of my might and shook my gun with my toothpick arms as intimidatingly as I could. But it was as useless as screaming in a dream; he looked at me coldly and said nothing. I don't know how or why I didn't pull the trigger.

"He was mine! I told you he was mine! Why did you do that? I told you I would die!" I kept yelling, repeating the same words over and over again.

As easily as I could have killed this officer, he could have killed me. There was a sense of panic in the other soldiers as they trained their guns to me and looked back to the officer to await orders. But he just stared forward at me and put his pistol back into his holster. It would have been foolish for more life to be lost over a killer. But in that moment, I would have done anything. *Perhaps by tugging that trigger,* I thought, *I would get my moment back, or somehow feel the closure I had sought for my father.* But something stopped me.

Finally I stopped yelling, I was out of things to say, and I just stared at him incredulously. He stood firm, and after the moment passed, he spoke. "Son," he said, "I did this for you. I can tell those in Tripoli that I shot him because he tried to escape. One day, you'll understand. Now go back and tell everyone he never made it to court."

My prized machine gun never fired a shot. I turned my head and walked back home, and as it hung from my arm, it felt like a heavy consolation prize. I wondered, quietly, if my father was proud.

CHAPTER 9

Relief

For the first time in years, I saw a truck, clanking up the road, kicking up dust. It reminded me of a sweeter time, when that old truck once brought my father and the wonderful treats from Tripoli that would stock his store. But that was a happier time, when I was a child untouched by war. This truck that I heard now was not the same. Through the Marshall Plan and the Truman Doctrine, America had launched a multiphase effort to help Europe and Greece recover from the destruction wrought during World War II. It yielded the first substantive relief that our families had seen in years.

Tons of food, clothes, and medications were pouring into Greece, and they eventually found their way to us, arriving in truckloads that evoked those blissful days when my father would return home after his long journeys. I can still see the villagers lining up and loading on their shoulders a bag of flour, rushing home eagerly to bake and eat white bread that they hadn't tasted for years.

Across the country, farmers received tractors and other farming machinery so they could cultivate their land. In Valtesiniko, where the difficult mountain terrain rendered such machinery useless, mules were sent. They were big and strong and pulled the plows, and as the lands slowly regained their vitality, the farmers did too.

Our family, too, was finding relief from America. My mother had two brothers, Dmitri and Anastasi, who had immigrated to America many years prior to the war. They wrote to her frequently, signing their letters with their chosen "American" names, Jimmy and George. I can remember how happy she would be, in the days before

51

the war, when my father was still alive, every time she received one of their letters.

My father would bring the letter to her, and her face would light up, and she would scurry off to a chair in our living room, pouring over their writing with an unconscious, closed-lip smile. Their exploits in a foreign land would make for riveting dinner conversation, and I could see my father listening intently, undoubtedly reliving his own cross-Atlantic romp.

It had been some time since I had seen that soft smile on my mother's face. During the war, under both the German and the communist occupations, all communications between Greece and the rest of the world were cut off. My mother had gone for years without hearing from her brothers until the Allies liberated us in 1945. That's when a telegram came from Uncles Jimmy and George, reading, simply, "Everybody is well here. Let us know of everyone's health there."

This was the first time I had seen my mother really cry since my father died despite all we had been through. She didn't cry often. But now, with a sense of material peace, this telegram seemed to bring everything forward. She was sobbing over these simple words.

She immediately tried to respond to them, to let them know all that had happened, to tell them that we were broken, but alive. But her tears were like rain on the paper, and she would intermittently stop to sob. It was a powerful emotional flood of happiness and tragedy. Finally, my older sister had to finish the letter for her. My mother had held back her pain for so long for the sake of all of us, for all the work that needed to be done. I think that getting that telegram was a release; it was an overwhelming blast of relief and despair, a realization that life had moved on even without her husband, that there were still joys to be found and sorrows to recount.

And now, with those trucks coming to Valtesiniko with food and clothes and red, white, and blue flags being waved all around, it felt that America was coming to our rescue, and our uncles were no exception. Soon our family began receiving packages with food and clothes from Uncles Jimmy and George. My mother slowly began returning to her pre-war routine of consuming their letters, scurrying off to find a quiet reprieve in their words.

Slowly, the hunger and poverty started to subside. But as our new normal life began to settle in, my world felt more fractured than it ever had before. Things could never go back to the way they were. I was a teenager at this point, and I had outgrown, or missed completely, the joys of youth. I just couldn't imagine myself taking bicycle rides or playing games with my friends or even laughing. And I got the sense that much of our village felt the same way.

On the surface, things seemed to be normal again, but the stain of the communists could never be removed. There had been too much betrayal and pain, and mistrust was sewed deeply into our hearts. I noticed a cynicism in the way people acted, less sincerity in their greetings, and a more protective, self-consumed attitude glinting in our eyes. Our big village family didn't feel the same anymore, and I silently begrudged the fact that all of the good people in our village who could have fixed it had been killed.

And even though the war had ended, there were still tragedies. Shortly after my mother began receiving their correspondences, she received a letter from Uncle George, informing her that her brother Jimmy had died unexpectedly of a heart attack. They hadn't seen each other since they were children.

She cried a lot after that, often without warning, and she became quiet and sad. She also became more overprotective of us than ever before, and she worried about me more than anyone.

While I had clothes on my back and food in my belly, my heart was still turning and my focus had not changed. Somewhere out there, Stasinopoulos roamed free while my father was dead. In these new, darker days, I was still clouded with anger, and I found myself longing to hear more about my father's youth, his adventures in America. I would never know his story, and the man responsible for that was still free.

Additionally, word had spread that I was somehow responsible for Kokkinis's death. There's no keeping secrets in a small village like ours, and I never tried to deny it either. While no one ever knew the full story, the rumors were enough to excite, perplex, and anger some. My mother never said a word of it to me, but I knew her increasingly watchful eye was no coincidence. I knew I couldn't hide my despair from her, no matter how I tried, and I'd guess that she could see that I had never quite returned to my childish place of innocence once the war ended.

One day, I found a rare moment when my mother wasn't watching and snuck into the crawl space in the wall and got the little machine gun, which I hadn't looked at since Kokkinis's death. It felt familiar in my hands, and I silently hoped that I would finally pull its trigger; I placed it into a bag and set out on a long walk from Valtesiniko to the town of Tropea, which I had heard from some villagers was Stasinopoulos's hometown. I didn't know if he was still there, but I had to look for myself.

I walked for hours and finally arrived as the sun had already moved past its peak. I was still a young and angry kid and I made a foolhardy mistake of approaching two strangers, asking them if they knew where Christo Stasinopoulos lived.

They got very suspicious of a stranger kid asking about a well-known killer, and they demanded to know who I was and where I came from. I tried to ignore them, but they became very persistent. I realized that I had made a mistake, and I kept my mouth shut, suspecting that these people may be his relatives or friends. I started to walk away and got ready to reach for my friend in my bag in case they followed me. Luckily, they didn't, and I took the long way back home.

When I returned, I was a bit shaken by the thought that I might have shot those men had they continued after me. I would have never been able to live with myself if I did and found out that they were just curious bystanders. I was grateful that my paranoia and rage didn't lead me to something that would have brought me to a dark place that I could never come back from.

I got home around midnight and made up some lie to my mother about where I had been. I could see the panic in her eye, and she scolded me harshly for leaving. She didn't press me about where I went; I don't think she really wanted to know. But she made clear that I was not to leave her sight for long again. She knew the rage inside my heart, and I think it scared her. I got the sense that she was feeling like Cleri the cat on the night before my father died, clawing wildly, doing anything she could to stop what felt like an inevitable onslaught of tragedy.

As deeply as my heart was hurting, I couldn't leave my mother like this, and soon I decided to let my hunt for Stasinopoulos wind down for her sake. My drive had diminished little; I still stared at the ceiling deep into the night, imagining the moment when I came face-to-face with him. But it became clear that as long as my mother was around, I could never venture out so far again. I tried to give up my quest for Stasinopoulos and tried to take solace in the role that I had in Kokkinis's death. But it wasn't enough; after all, it was Stasinopoulos who fired the gun that killed my father. I felt sad and empty, and my days grew longer and less meaningful.

Things dragged on for years. One day, my mother got a letter from Uncle George. He had recently learned that he was allowed to sponsor one relative from Greece and was asking my mother if she wanted to send any of her kids to America, where a job would be waiting for them so they could send money back home.

My mother hardly thought about the decision. That day, she called me over and showed me the letter and told me that she wanted me to go. I was seventeen at the time, and I wasn't so keen on the idea at first; it didn't make sense to me that I should go when my older brother could be so much more productive than me. I was also confused as to why my mother, who had been watching me like a hawk, was so willing to let me sail across the Atlantic. The reason was, of course, something I didn't realize at the time. They could see that Greece was no longer my home, at least, not in the way it once was. I had become an uneasy, irritated, and angry kid. They knew I would never let go of what had happened, and a life obsessed with blood for blood is no life at all. They believed that America could free me.

Years later, I found out there was even more to the story. My family had become increasingly concerned about my safety. Kokkinis, as hated as he was, still had family who loved him. I believe they saw him as a victim of circumstance, a puppet used by the communists to commit acts of evil. And while nobody would ever know the full extent of my involvement with his death, everyone knew how badly I wanted him dead.

Certainly, people had their suspicions, and my family feared that someone from Kokkinis's family might come to me, point a gun in my face, and seek their own revenge. My family knew something that I didn't yet understand: that my hatred was not unique but inherited. And by trying to act on it, I had inevitably passed it down to someone else. I was just another episode in a cycle of violence and killing that has perpetuated itself since long before my time on earth.

At the time, I'm sure I would have never accepted their concerns. I felt that I had done an honorable thing and shouldn't run from it. Even today, I don't regret my actions; I simply understand them as part of my journey.

My mother desperately implored me to take Uncle George up on his offer, and soon I felt that staying to seek out my revenge would break her heart. And so, with a bitter heart, I decided to immigrate to America.

The idea of America carried all the mysteries of my father. I can see his smile as he spoke of it, just after the rebels asserted their power over us. It was freedom. It had to be freedom. And if I couldn't get my revenge, the thought of America was the only thing that would keep me sane, the idea that this journey would grant me freedom from painful weights that kept me shackled to a broken home. As I've grown, I've realized that my father was not the kind of man who cared for bloodlust, and I believe he would have hated the angry person that I was on the verge of becoming. I didn't realize it at the time that I made my decision to leave, but my hate had obscured my true purpose: to follow the path that my father had always wanted for me.

CHAPTER 10

The Italia—Crossing the Atlantic with Elias

I began my journey to America at the age of seventeen on January 11, 1952. It was a bitterly cold morning. Snow was driven hard by the strong mountain wind. I had to ride on a truck to Tripoli then travel by bus to a coastal city of Patra and board an Italian sea liner called the *Italia* that was to carry hundreds of hopeful immigrants to America. Only my brother was able to come and see me off.

The day before, I took out of its hiding place the little machine gun and hid it under the pulpit of St. Barbara's Church. The church is a very short distance from the spot where my father was killed, and even closer to the house of Kapelianis, our neighbor, who Stasinopoulos shot in his bed just moments after he shot my father. It felt appropriate. It was an apology of sorts, to both of them, a private reminder of my failure to enact justice, a monument of my efforts to do so, and a promise that I would try again if I ever returned. I only told George, a boy of my age, the son of our neighbor Kapelianis, who had also watched his father being shot. I am sure he felt the same I was feeling for years, and I would let him decide what to do with that gun. I wanted to let him know that there was a friend if he ever needed one.

The next day, before leaving, my mother gave me a strong bear hug and wouldn't let go, and my sisters followed. I tried to be strong. In recent years, I had developed a reputation as a cold, emotionless young man, and I intended to keep it that way. But the pain and fear of leaving was too much, and soon, even I shed some tears. I had vowed to never cry again after my father died, and until that day, seven years later, I had kept that promise.

In today's world, I don't think there's a true appreciation for the words "goodbye." I suppose that's because there really is no such thing anymore. We are all so connected; someone's moving to the other side of the planet doesn't stop us from picking up the phone, writing an e-mail, or sharing pictures and well wishes as instantly as if we were sitting right there with them. But in those days, "good-bye" carried with it a sense of permanence. It was not a word that we threw around so carelessly.

In this house, I would become like my uncles, an occasional piece of paper that arrived in the mail many weeks later. I hoped I would bring my mother as much joy as they did. I knew that when I boarded that boat, it would be many years before I would see my family again. And so I took their faces in, held them tightly, and allowed myself to spend the tears.

I carried a small bag tossed over my shoulder with some clothes that I had, and when my brother and I climbed into the back of the truck, the freezing weather overtook us, and we started shivering like leaves in the wind. But just before the truck pulled away, a sympathetic shepherd took off his homemade sheepskin coat and tossed it up to us, and immediately its strong, bad, lamb smell took our breath away. We had a choice to make: it was either the bad smell or freeze. I don't know how we would have made that trip to Tripoli without that furry smelly coat.

That shepherd handing me the coat off his back was my last parting memory of Valtesiniko, whose people were broken, but a family, nonetheless.

Fortunately, the bus from Tripoli to Patra was warm, so I tucked the coat into my bag. We arrived in Patra in the early afternoon, and I said goodbye to my brother, but as I boarded the *Italia* and looked back at him, I felt a sudden longing to turn around and go home. I don't know what kept my legs moving forward. It was a sense, I suppose, that my decision had already been made and could not be unmade, like when you step outside without a key for a moment, just to feel the air, and an unexpected gust slams the door behind you. I felt, for some reason, like any attempt to turn around would be futile.

Aboard the *Italia*, I had many thoughts. My family was still rebuilding itself, straddling the line between poverty and comfort as Stasinopoulos still breathed. Ostensibly, I was starting a new life, but truly, I felt that I was simply pausing my old one. I tried to tell myself that, one day, Stasinopoulos would feel like a distant echo, that life would provide joys much more fulfilling than riding a bike through a flock of sheep. But I would never believe it until I saw it. I boarded that ship with a bag filled with little and a head filled with doubts.

As the *Italia* chugged out of the harbor and Patra's skyline disappeared, I tried not to think of the uncertainty of my life, but all I could see was sky and water for miles, as waves rocked our ship. This is my life, I thought, a turbulent, unknown horizon.

But there was one shining star that guided me, a memory that I had never let go of. That word *America* and how it sounded as it fell from my father's mouth. It fascinated me. It was a word that I had come to equate with freedom and peace, without really ever understanding why. It seemed to be my father's heaven, a place where his imagination took him when life became too hard. I often imagined it as a heaven of my own, in a sense, and as I stared out to sea at the beginning of my journey, I wondered if my father would be on the other side.

Little did I know that it wasn't my father, or Jesus, or Saint Peter, or God waiting for me. It was Audie Murphy, Frank Sinatra, George Steinbrenner, Anthony Quinn, and Muhammad Ali.

The *Italia* was packed full of passengers like me—all victims of the civil war seeking work in America to help the families we were leaving behind. Prior to that day, I had never seen an ocean or been on a boat, and when the Italia entered the Atlantic Ocean, it was bobbing up and down so violently that it made me sick to my stomach, and I rushed below to my cabin where my sickness got worse.

I shared a cabin with another boy my age by the name of Elias Sitilides from the northern part of Greece. Although Elias and I came from different regions of Greece, we became perfect roommates and fast friends. I remember my first night, as I lay on my bunk seasick, with my stomach on a rampage and the dilapidated condition of the *Italia* doing little to help. It was a small old ship, powered by noisy engines that made the cabins smell like diesel fuel, and it was Elias who first got me to eat; he brought me food from up above and encouraged me to get up and walk around.

"A mountain boy like me has no business here," I told him.

"Me either. Let's jump off and swim back…" Elias replied jokingly, knowing that neither of us could swim.

But he was persistent and always willing to help. Perhaps he just didn't want to see me throwing up all over the cabin. He kept pushing me to go up on deck and get some fresh air, promising that it would make me feel better. Finally, I worked up some strength to stand up and start making my way outside. With Elias leading the way, I slowly put one foot in front of the other from my cot to the staircase. But once we started climbing the stairs, the seas became rougher, and the ship lurched forward, launching us into the wall and onto the ground like dice rolled onto a craps table. When I tried to stand up, my resolve broke, and I threw up all over. That would be the end of my adventures for the day.

Elias, glad that I threw up in the staircase and not in our cabin, helped my back into my cot. I lay there awake, hardly moving, willing the seas to stay calm and wishing I was back in Valtesiniko where the mountains were sturdy and still.

The next morning, I was feeling a little better, and I decided that I should try to go upstairs to eat some real food. So finally, with Elias's help, I managed to climb the steps and enter the dining room. There, I couldn't help but notice tension among my fellow travelers, and as I looked closer, I could see the scars we all bore, the faces that bore witness to the killings, the poverty and pain.

They all kept to themselves in their own little circles, very somber, puffing on their cigarettes, and talking in hushed conversations. In those very few moments, I had understood their stories and I could see on their faces familiar scars. Perhaps our stories weren't precisely the same, but they came from the same author: civil war.

I began to see a strand running through all of us there, and I realized that we were all, literally, in the same boat. I took an uneasy comfort in their dark faces as I sat down at the same table with Elias and four other youngsters my age that all seemed to know one another. I had missed all of the first day's meals and felt like I was playing catch up on making friends.

Elias introduced me to them, but I was distracted with little bottles on the table filled with a dark liquid with a deep red undertone. I had never seen it before. At the tables around us, wine was being served, but us kids only had these little bottles.

When one of the other kids opened one, it made a popping sound, and some spilled out onto the table. Elias offered me an open one, but I hesitated. Then he explained to me it was a drink called Coca-Cola, and it was okay for us to drink it. I brought the bottle to my lips and felt the bubbly liquid tickle my tongue. I loved it, and I made a note in my head to tell my family about the drink in my first letter to them.

It was my third day aboard the *Italia*, I was finally feeling better, and we were sitting with the other boys at a dining room table to eat, when a waiter addressed me, calling me "sir." I was floored; I initially thought it was some sarcastic joke, and I almost pounced on him. But then he said it again, and I gave him a stern look of warning that he ignored. Each time he came over, he would call me sir again. But each time, I noticed the same sincerity in his voice.

I didn't feel like a "sir." Frankly, I could count on one hand the number of "sirs" I had met in my entire life. If he had seen me standing with that gun geared toward Kokkinis with a killer's look in my face, I don't believe he would call me "sir."

Somehow, I was happy he hadn't seen me then because each time he called me "sir," I began to feel calm and comfortable. For the first time in my life, I felt important, and I would embrace it for as long as I could.

Strangely, I felt that this stranger had taught me something I never knew, something good, something important, that made me, in that brief moment, a better person. And the next time he came around, I called him "sir" too. He accepted it, smiling. I've held that

61

moment closely to my heart. It was a rare moment where I could feel my own humanity in a time that I often felt I was observing my actions from outside my body. And to happen in a place as dark and desperate as the *Italia* was a miracle.

Slowly, my seasickness started to pass, and for the first time in three days, food tasted good to me. I clung to my Coca-Cola happily when suddenly, a large wave smashed against the *Italia*, and everything got tossed around like little toys. It happened so quickly, and no one had a chance to react. There was a panic all over, people were screaming, and many lunged over to grab onto one another as tables overturned, sending dishes with food and dishes flying everywhere. It felt like we were in a big earthquake, and with the thought of that flat unknown horizon extending out beyond us in all directions, each creak in the boat's hull was terrifying. I don't know how long it lasted, but it felt like forever, and we had no way of knowing what would come next.

This was a new fear for all of us; we all had seen and faced death, and some of us had felt the fury of a bullet whizzing by, and we knew how quickly it could end. But never before had any of us been at the mercy of the sheer force of our planet like this. Most of the passengers were like me, living on the mountains with no sign of the ocean for miles, and the idea of drowning in that dark abyss was a terror that we had only read about. At those moments, I would have much rather preferred the bullet, and I'm sure that my terrified shipmates would feel the same.

At one point, the floor seemed to be stable again, and as we tried to get up, we noticed one unopened wine bottle had settled nearby. I picked it up and handed it to Elias, and when finally managed to get our table to stay still, Elias open the bottle and took a couple of swigs. Then he passed it to me, and after a good swallow, I gave it to the boy next to me. The bottle kept traveling around the group with each of us stealthily taking hearty swigs until it was empty.

As the boat continued to sway, I could no longer tell if it was from the waves or the wine. I looked around still and saw a sense of unease, a fear that another wave will soon come and finish us off, sending the *Italia* to the bottom of the ocean floor. But my young friends and I had not a care in the world, having just discovered the healing properties of wine.

As the boat kept rocking, everyone continued clutching one another, expecting the worst. Suddenly, Elias stood up and broke into a song, some popular song at the time about sailors crossing the ocean. It was the stereotypical kind of sea shanty, I'm sure. Elias had a strong, smooth voice, but it was his vigor and the smile on his face that caught everyone's attention, and all the desperate, scared heads turned to look at him.

I remember those magical moments. It was as if everyone on the ship was waiting for something like this to happen, and soon, all of the faces turned to smiles as Elias's voice filled the room. It felt like everyone's fear disappeared, and even as the *Italia* kept rocking, there was a soothing sense that all would be okay.

One by one, they picked up their bottles of wine and gathered around Elias, and they all started to sing along with him. Soon the entire room began to vibrate with singing voices. Like a magician, Elias and his song transformed a room full of frightened strangers into a makeshift band of happy travelers who would prefer to drown while singing rather than crying.

When the song finished, the room was loud with laughter as we exchanged names, shared stories, and talked of our dreams. We spoke of the war and our experiences and our hopes that we could leave it all behind us. We kept on singing and drinking all night, telling those ferocious waves that we were not afraid anymore.

The revelry did nothing to stop the waves from crashing into the boat, and I can't remember when the boat stopped rocking, if it ever did. But soon, everyone seemed to stop caring. I think that singing made us all realize that being on that boat was not all that different from our own lives, filled with fear, violence, and uncertainty, but still capable of these beautiful moments of joy. We could never stop the waves, but we could still find hope.

Elias and his song had made us into the warriors who accompanied Odysseus on his journey home, celebrating our victories in Troy, unaware of the detours our journey would take. But we had decidedly more positive outlooks than those men. After all, we weren't celebrating victory, per se, but tragedy, and after tragedy, there's nowhere to go but up. And the homes that we were sailing to were not familiar plots of lands. For many of us, it was a home that we had yet to create, with a future that was still uncertain. And that night, I felt that a little uncertainty could do me a lot of good.

It took eleven days and eleven nights to cross the Atlantic Ocean and to reach America. And after the first two days and nights, the rest of the way was nothing but a happy journey. Every night, we'd all gather to listen to Elias sing his songs, and we'd let him take away our pain, foster our brotherhood, and slowly, we tried to force ourselves to learn how to trust again. Like the sheepskin coat that helped my brother and I survive our trip to Tripoli, it was Elias who helped us survive the Italia when times got dark.

I was luckier than most; sharing a cabin with him gave me the opportunity to create a lifelong friendship with Elias. Like any lifelong friendship, there were years apart. But we reconnected again one day in Astoria, Queens's Greek enclave in New York City. By that time, Elias had created a loving family with a wonderful lady named Fotinoula and two sons named John and George. We would see each other often, never forgetting where we came from, especially those eleven days and eleven nights at sea, and how Elias would sing when the occasion arose, bringing us all peace and ease. I was very saddened with his death in 2016.

An entire ship's worth of scared immigrants have him to thank. While it was the *Italia* that carried us, Elias was the man who brought us to America.

11 days on the ITALIA

CHAPTER 11

America, America

On the morning of January 22, 1952, after eleven nights and eleven days at sea, the New York skyline appeared in the distance. It was a sight that had been recounted to me in letters and in pictures, a portrait of steel, a gateway to a new world. It was something that I had longed to see since the day I boarded the *Italia*, and as soon as word spread that we were approaching, everyone began to shuffle up to the deck.

As the Italia entered the New York harbor, the deck was already crowded, and what had started as a chatty and energetic gathering turned into something quiet and still. My eyes turned to the Statue of Liberty, and I quickly recognized it from stories my father would tell us of "the statue in the harbor." But in person I could feel its magic; it seemed so real, like its eyes were scanning the horizon on a steadfast watch, welcoming us with a warm and dutiful face.

Out past the statue, Manhattan's west side came into view, comprising the tallest buildings I had ever seen. They struck me dumb and appeared to me as a miracle; I imagined that it's a feeling similar to how the disciples felt when they saw Jesus walk out across the water. When my father would tell me about those "skyscrapers," I never imagined it would be that different from the modest urban sprawl of Tripoli or Patra. No stories had prepared me for this; it was beyond imagination.

I noticed the clouds, as they appeared to pass by the tops of the tallest buildings. Never had I seen the feats of man reach so close to the heavens, and I understood why my father had used that word:

"skyscrapers." Even our pine trees, which as a child, always appeared to scrape the sky, seemed like mere blades of grass compared to these giants.

I stood still with my eyes fixed, unblinking, fearing that I would miss something, on the sprawling metropolis before me. No one said a word, but it didn't feel silent. There was a busy energy in the air that my father had never mentioned to me. Even from the boat I could see that the city was alive like an anthill, and as we got closer, I could see the West Side highway crawling with automobiles. How could there be so many on one street? In Valtesiniko, I would only see that lone truck coming and going along the narrow dirt road every couple of days at most. And on the major roads, maybe you could see an automobile once every few hours.

In fact, my initial instinct was fear; the only time I had ever seen so many automobiles together in one place was when the Germans led their armies across Greece.

"It must be some kind of military caravan!" I heard one of my co-travelers say, echoing my thoughts.

But we were both wrong. It was just another day of traffic in New York City.

I was also stunned by the strange wires that seemed to float above all of the rooftops. I turned to one of the crewmen and asked what they were.

"Those are television antennas," he said before walking away.

But his answer only left me more confused. I was only vaguely aware of what a television was. Some of us might have heard of a device that showed people from one city to people in another city, but none of us had any idea of how those magic boxes worked. It sounded like a fairy tale, but now I was seeing the evidence apparently, tied from the litany of rooftops dotting the blocks of the city. I wondered how they worked, how those moving pictures of people zoomed across those wires and played out on the screen.

In front of me was an entire world that was foreign and strange, and as I stared at it, there was a knot in my stomach, and I started to wonder. What kinds of people live here? Are the people in this land as different as the buildings? Can so many people live here peacefully? And how would I have to change to live among them? My mind was a whirl of wondering and doubts.

Then it happened.

As the *Italia* entered pier 76, the initial shock of the foreign left me, and suddenly I was possessed with new strange feelings.

There was a warm sense of adventure that I hadn't felt since I was a kid, romping around the countryside and flying through flocks of sheep. And as I processed how different everything was, my horrifying memories of all that had happened, the German occupation, the communist tyranny, the death of my father, the hate and anger, it all felt muted somehow. It had all magically become the lore of some ancient civilization, some past version of me that I had only seen glimpses of in dreams. I felt as though I had just finished a prison sentence, and now, the heavy gates had opened before me, and I stood outside a free man. I'd never completely forget the pain of the past, but for now at least, there were new adventures to embark on.

It was a transcendent feeling, and for a moment I believed I was dreaming. But then I began to smile, knowing that I had just entered a new, beautiful world, and most importantly, a world that was far more liberating than the one I once knew. And as I looked around at the faces of my newly found friends on the *Italia*, I noticed that each one of them shared that same dumb smile.

I knew then, that we were all experiencing the same feelings.

As we docked, I rushed to get my bag, and we all scrambled to grab one another by the arm and say our goodbyes. We shared any information that we could use to find eachother after we'd all found ourselves. We shook hands, congratulating one another, I suppose, for accomplishing some hazy, ill-defined feat. It felt like a celebration, a going-away, and welcome-home party all in one.

Eleven days and eleven nights, that's how long it took for hundreds of immigrants' lives to change forever, including mine.

CHAPTER 12

Uncle George

In those days, to come to America you needed a sponsor, a person who was an American citizen, who could be accountable for you during your first few years, a person who would give you a place to stay, help you get a job, get established and, most importantly, teach you how to blend in and adapt to life in America. For me, this person was my Uncle George.

Uncle George had immigrated to America many years before I was born, and I had never met him. I only knew him from his letters and the stories my mother would tell us around the dinner table. She always talked about him as a short man, and I remember finding comfort in that, because as a child, I had been so small and scrawny myself.

My mother fondly said that what he lacked in height, God replaced with kindness. She described him as a jolly man, always smiling with a toothy grin, and always making people laugh. He wore that smile in the photograph that my mother showed me so that I would recognize him when I stepped foot in America.

When the *Italia* docked into pier 76, I was immediately excited and anxious to meet Uncle George, but instead, I was met with a long and winding line of immigrants being processed before disembarking. It was a long process as one by one, we had to step in front a desk and speak to the processing officer through an interpreter to get clearance, then the officer would call out our sponsor's name over a loudspeaker to come forward to a waiting area to meet us, and after that, it was a long walk on a ramp down to the waiting area.

However, the line trudged along slowly, and there was a freezing gust blowing in from the river, and we all got closer to one another to keep warm. I reached into my bag and pulled out the wooly sheepskin coat the village shepherd had given me and put it on. I paid no attention to the strange looks I was getting from the people around me. I didn't care as long as I was warm. But soon I found myself standing in line all alone; the strong smell of the coat had forced everyone away, and I could see them all, staring at me. Finally I reached the desk where I got more strange looks from the processing staff who speeded up the process to get me through quickly.

I got my clearance, and I walked down the ramp, still wearing the sheepskin coat and my bag hanging off my shoulder, still getting funny looks from the people standing around waiting. I heard my uncle's name called, and I saw a little man step out from the waiting crowd, walking toward me.

I recognized him, and I picked up my pace as I walked toward him, anxious and excited to meet him, but as I approached, Uncle George stopped suddenly and started to look over my shoulders, his eyes squinting, as if he were looking for something behind me.

I stopped just in front of him, dropped my bag to the ground, and extended my arms, expecting a warm handshake and a hug, a hearty laugh, and that toothy grin that he had in the picture my mother had given me. But none of that happened. Uncle George kept looking over my shoulders, still looking to see something behind me.

For a moment, I thought that maybe I had found the wrong person, or that he thought I was someone else and he was looking behind me to see if he could spot the real Dino. But then I noticed his eyes skirting over to me as he looked me up and down, taking note of my sheepskin coat. Finally, he took one more look behind me and threw his arms up into the air, feigning disappointment. "Well? Where are your sheep?" he asked loudly, and the people around waiting broke into a loud laughter. I looked over, and I saw they were all looking at me, laughing. At that moment, I remember wishing there was a hole nearby for me to jump into.

In my village, coats like these were a common sight, and I had no idea that it would be such a strange item to wear in America.

Uncle George was laughing also, and I could see that toothy smile and the sense of humor that I had heard so much about. Although I was embarrassed, I considered it my official welcome to America, and as the laughter continued, Uncle George shook my hand and embraced me, but the smell of my coat forced him to pull away quickly.

Happy to meet Uncle George, I picked up my bag and followed Uncle George about two blocks, thinking we were going to board a bus or a train to get to his home in Elizabeth, New Jersey. But soon we approached a parked car, and I was surprised when he opened its trunk. Before we got into the car, Uncle George asked me to take off the coat and put it into the trunk. The car was an old Desoto with the gearshift on its floor and a little fan on the dashboard. I had never been inside a car before, and to me it was like I had entered something luxurious that I had never dreamed of before.

I became dazed, staring out the car's window as it rolled through New York City's big streets and roomy sidewalks, the flood of cars and the chorus of honking, the streams of people walking alongside one another. The winding dirt roads of our mountain village had now been replaced with concrete paths, straight as an arrow and arranged in perfect squares. The tall pine trees were replaced with these giant skyscrapers, which forced me to strain my neck to see their tops.

Traveling through the wide streets of New York, Uncle George kept asking me all kinds of questions about the family, the village, and all that had happened, but I was distracted by the wonders of the modern world that I had only heard of in stories that always seemed to me nothing more than legends, and I don't remember how I answered him. I was daydreaming now, imagining ways that I could become part of this daily circuit. It was amazing to me that so many cars and so many people could all coexist, carrying out their own respective tasks for their own respective lives.

Everything here was different; everyone seemed so set on their own lives and coexisting with each other. There was something beautiful in it, a sense that one could carve out their own destiny, write their own story. I grew excited, imagining myself in Uncle George's seat, in my own car, driving to my own job and later returning to my own home, sending my earnings to my family back home.

But my sweet daydream suddenly turned into a nightmare as we entered a long dark tunnel, and I got very nervous, and I asked Uncle George what that was and why we were in there. He explained it was the Lincoln Tunnel, which was built under the harbor's waters, beneath where the *Italia* had passed just hours earlier. His response terrified me. The thought that I was enclosed beneath miles and miles of ocean, the same ocean that I had only recently just become acquainted with, was too much for me. I started having a difficult time catching my breath, praying to emerge from the tunnel quickly.

I couldn't quite wrap my head around the concept, and part of me doubted that it was possible. I wished my father had warned me about this. The little he had told me about America was always about its people and the vague idea of freedom that meant so much to me. He never told me about the inhuman feats that man had reached as Greece stayed tethered to the mountains and the farms.

I recalled that thrill of the bicycle again, the mystery of how it worked, how its mechanical gears transformed the pressure of my foot into forward motion. It wasn't that different from the car that I sat in now as I watched Uncle George press and release his foot from the gas. But now we were going five times as fast, racing below the oceans. My bicycle suddenly seemed to me a trinket.

"Don't worry. Once I felt the same way also," Uncle George said, smiling when we finally got out of that tunnel.

Until we reached Uncle George's house, I was fascinated traveling on the New Jersey turnpike, how spacious and smooth with so many cars traveling in both directions.

When I arrived, I was welcomed by a smiling, 100 percent Greek lady, Aunt Eleni, and their little six-year-old son, my cousin Kimon, a kind of bratty kid who showed me how much he disliked me from the moment I stepped into the house. From that moment, he never called me by name, always referring to me as the "Greek Boy." They also had an older son named Costas. He was a pharmacist and was serving as a medic on Korea's front lines. That had Aunt Eleni and Uncle George worrying every minute.

On my second day at Uncle George's house, he took me and Kimon on a stroll to nearby Broad Street, which was the center of life in Elizabeth. Like a tour guide, he ushered me around all the major stops in the area, as I craned my neck in every direction to take everything in. We saw the supermarket, the drugstore, the candy store, the barber shop. He explained to me how the crosswalk lights worked to ensure that I wouldn't be hit by one of those cars that fascinated me. The tour did little to improve my relationship with Kimon, as I could see in his face that he was impatient and confused, unsure why his father was guiding us on a tour of what were, to him, the mundane amenities of life. Surely it befuddled him to see a seventeen-year-old who had never seen a crossing light before.

The following Sunday, we went to church, and when we returned home, Uncle George asked me if I remembered the candy store we'd passed on Broad Street, and I told him yes. Then he gave me two silver coins and told me to go there. "You don't have to say anything," he said. "Just put these coins in the plate by the window and pick up the paper called the *New York Times* and bring it to me." He even wrote "New York Times" on a piece of paper and gave it to me, making sure I would find it.

I was very happy that my uncle would ask me to do something for him. After all, I felt I owed him so much. But as I left the house, I began to fill with adrenaline. I was nervous about navigating the streets, which, while straight and smoothly paved and labeled with street signs, were more complicated than the familiar winding roads in Valtesiniko. But more importantly, I began to suspect that this might be a test, that my uncle was trying to see how well his tour had stuck with me. I felt a strong urge to impress him, to show him I was a fast learner and capable of accomplishing basic tasks without complication. I'd better do this well, I told myself.

I had no trouble finding the candy store, which was about three or four blocks away. I placed the two quarters at the counter and turned to the shelves of newspapers. There were so many newspapers in there, and it took me a minute or two to spot the pile that said "New York Times," as my uncle had written down for me. All the while, the man inside the window was looking at me.

73

I picked up the paper and was surprised by its weight and thickness of more than two inches. I remember in Greece, the major newspapers we had were very light, at only four or six pages. This big bundle that I was holding must have been for the whole town of Elizabeth, I thought. So to avoid any embarrassment, I put the papers down, peeled off the first six pages, and started back home, happy that I had accomplished my first chore in America.

I went home and handed Uncle George his newspaper. He looked at me with eyes wide open and raised his hands up in the air, much like how he did back in New York when he saw me with my sheepskin coat. I thought he was about to make a joke, and I pre-emptively laughed.

"What is this?" he said. "Where is the rest of it?"

For little Kimon this was hysterical, and he started to laugh, pointing at me and cackling, like he had been waiting for something like this to happen. I became embarrassed, still not completely aware of what exactly had made my little cousin laugh so hard at me. I wanted him to stop laughing, but he just wouldn't until Uncle George finally snapped at him. He told me to take Kimon by the hand and walk back to the candy store, where Kimon could explain to the man what had happened and take the rest of the paper and bring it back to him.

But for Kimon, this was a dream come true, and he couldn't wait to get there. He was yanking at my hand, pulling at me to move faster, and when we finally arrived at the candy store, this kid opened up his mouth, rushed to tell the man at the store his story. He spoke so quickly; he sounded like an auctioneer. I couldn't understand what he was saying; he was pointing at me saying: "Greek Boy," along with a new word to me: "stupid." And they both started to laugh while I stood there, trying to figure out what was going on.

By now, I only knew what the two words, "Greek Boy," meant, but I had no idea what the word "stupid" meant, and I stood there wondering, feeling frustrated. Finally, the man must have realized my frustrations and handed me the remains of the newspaper with a motion to leave.

On the way back home, I couldn't forget that word, "stupid," that had made the man and Kimon laugh so much, and I decided that I had to find out what it meant. In those days, words like "stupid" were not in everyday, usual conversation. In fact, it was considered to be a very harsh and mean word, and when I asked Uncle George what "stupid" meant, he became appalled that I had uttered such a word.

"Where did you hear that?" he asked me, very surprised. I explained to him what had happened.

He smiled a little, then he took a serious pose and asked again, "Do you really want to know what that means?"

"Yes," I told him. "I want to know."

Uncle George looked me straight in the eyes and shook his finger in front of my face, saying, "It means you must learn to speak English so you won't need a six-year-old as an interpreter just to buy a newspaper."

That was one of the many wise pieces of advice my uncle George gave me that helped me create a better life in America.

A few days later, he got me a job in a large bakery called Tempting Pies in the nearby town of Linden, New Jersey. It was a large place that produced all kind of pies and supplied them to diners all over the tristate area. The owners were Greek and good friends of my uncle who insisted that they talk to me in English so I learn the language. And that was how I first learned English.

My job there was an all-around helper. I worked six days a week at seventy-five cents an hour. I didn't really understand what that meant at first. All I knew was that I was working, and it felt good to be doing something and to be productive for the first time since I was a child. It was a nice distraction from the often-dark recesses of my thoughts, and for the first time in my life, I felt that I was working toward something. I had no idea what it was, but there was an end goal, and it didn't involve blood.

In those days, the employer cashed the paychecks and gave the employees cash in an envelope. I remember well the time I got my first envelope. When I went home, I opened it and counted thirty-nine dollars and forty cents. I figured out how much that would be in Greek drachmas and stood there in awe. I was rich.

I was eager to begin helping my family immediately, and by staying with my uncle, I had no expenses. So quickly, I started to send nearly all the money back to my family. One day, after I opened my envelope, Uncle George took me shopping for new clothes and shoes. I was excited to have new, warm things, especially in the frigid weather. But soon, my uncle told me that these new items were not for me. They were for the shepherd who gave me his sheepskin coat.

"Never forget someone who gives you the coat off his back," he told me.

Uncle George, Aunt Eleni and sons Costas & Kimon

CHAPTER 13

The Draft

Living at Uncle George's house was the beginning of my new life in America. Uncle George always found new ways to make me a part of his family, my aunt Eleni always found new ways to make me welcome, and my little cousin always found new ways to torture me. But in the end, I considered him as my little spoiled brother, and I didn't mind him. It was a house filled with love, something I hadn't experienced in a long time.

Meanwhile, I was happy working at the pie factory, making money and helping my family in Greece. I felt like I was fulfilling my purpose of coming to America, and soon, I started to get more comfortable speaking English and adjusting well to the new and better life I had found.

At the same time, America was engaged in the Korean War, and the country had been undergoing the draft. My other cousin, Costas, had already been drafted, and he'd been serving since before I arrived, so I never got the chance to meet him.

I started to note the sadness and sense of despair in my Uncle George's and Aunt Eleni's faces as they were anxiously watching the news on television. They didn't talk much about Costas, but there were nights when I could see them sitting, lost in thought, and I always imagined that their hearts were in Korea with their son. And there were the days when both would jump out of their skin at the sound of the telephone or the sound of the doorbell.

I was working at the factory for about a year when, one evening after work, I came home to a somber Uncle George and Aunt

Eleni. I could see the concern and sadness on their faces. Even little Kimon was sitting quiet watching cartoons on television. It was very unusual, and immediately I believed that they had received bad news from Korea. Finally, Uncle George broke the silence and told me that a letter had arrived from the draft board, instructing me to report to Elizabeth's armory for physical examinations.

"They won't accept you. You don't speak English well," Uncle George murmured wistfully.

The letter had not had the same effect on me as it did on Uncle George and Aunt Eleni. Instead, it awakened an old dream that had never really left me but had been dormant since I arrived in America. I thought of the day that the Allies entered Valtesiniko, and how, as a young child, I idolized those soldiers. They were our heroes, to be certain, but they were almost godlike to me at that age, like Titans from a distant land, crafted by some higher power of myth and legend.

As I held that little machine gun in my hand, dreaming of Stasinopoulos, I wanted so badly to join them. I remember day-dreams of entering into towns like ours and giving that same sense of peace and justice that they gave to my family. As I grew older, it became more of a fantasy, one that I had all but given up on when I boarded the *Italia*.

But now that dream felt more real than I could have ever imagined. Now I was a young man divided, caught between two opposing narratives. One born from the past, of glory and blood, of vengeance and death. The other from the future, of lawns and white fences and a family, a house, a dog and a cat, all the trappings of the American Dream. After only a year, was I so willing to abandon this emerging vision of peace?

I couldn't deny to myself that, in seeing that letter, my instinctual emotion was happiness, even relief. And as I saw the pain in my aunt and uncle's eyes, I felt guilty for feeling that way. But it made something very clear to me: perhaps I'd never be ready for the simple happiness of familial life. The pain of my early life was far too great to ever truly dissipate. It was always lingering, always a part of me.

Maybe this letter was the universe's way of reminding me that I was always a soldier at heart.

Sheepishly, I told Uncle George and Aunt Eleni how I felt, that I was excited about the opportunity, and that I hoped my English would not be a factor. They seemed very surprised, but I think, on some level, they understood. They had left Greece far before the violence started, and I think they knew that, had they been there, they may have felt the same way.

That week I reported promptly to the armory in Elizabeth, with the nervous approval of my American sponsor family. I went through many medical examinations, skating by with my broken English, which I anxiously hoped wouldn't stop me. Every minute, I grew more and more eager to see if I'd be accepted. A denial would feel like failure, and with every step I took toward this newly resurfaced dream, I grew more certain that it was the right path for me. Meanwhile, I looked around at the scared young men around me who wanted so desperately to have an excuse like poor English to avoid becoming soldiers. I felt guilty and could see how they all looked at me, yearning to trade places.

Luckily, the language barrier didn't matter. And when I boarded a bus for Fort Dix, New Jersey, I realized that, somehow, I had become part of the US Army. Still, there was one thing troubling me. By following this path, I knew that I was now unable to send as much money back to my family in Greece as I could before, working at Tempting Pies, and part of me was concerned that I had made a terrible selfish mistake.

Those feelings were not eased by the hellish treatment that me and the other rookies received upon arriving in Fort Dix. Still in civilian clothes, we were told firmly that we were no longer civilians. Rather, we were soldiers of the United States Army. We were told that we were no longer the sons of our fathers and mothers, but the sons of Uncle Sam. Then, we were all marched to a place where we stood in a long line to get our hair cut very short and were then brought to another place to get our Army uniforms.

We had a platoon Sergeant Slater, who seemed to take a twisted joy in ordering pushups as punishments when his orders weren't followed. He spoke with authority, loud and fast, and with a southern accent that was often difficult to understand, especially for me with my limited English. That meant that I was often on the receiving end of his harsh, punitive demeanor. If I misunderstood his order, or did it poorly, he would bark.

"Hey, Spaghetti," he would yell to me, referencing my skinny frame, "give me another twenty."

I think I spent more time facing the ground on my hands than standing up. That was until one day, Sergeant Slater ordered me to report to the company commander, Captain Waldman.

"This is it," I told myself. "I've messed up too much, misunderstood one too many orders." I was certain I was being kicked out of the Army.

I entered the captain's office, ready to hear the bad news; I snapped to attention and saluted him. He returned the salute and ordered me to "at ease" and gave me a smile. I was surprised to see that he had a much friendlier demeanor than Sergeant Slater. Looking at the papers on his desk, the captain started explaining to me that I had come to America as a war victim to work and help my family, and now I was drafted.

"I know all of this captain," I told myself, "please tell me why I am here."

Finally, to my relief, the captain went on to say that the Army had a program for soldiers in my situation and explained that as a rookie, my pay was $91 per month. But under this program, if I was willing to voluntarily donate $50 each month, the government would match that and send a total of $100 back to my family in Greece. I quickly did the calculations and realized that $100 dollars a month at that time in Greece could not only feed my family but many in our village. When the captain told me to think about it before signing the papers, I replied quickly. "I already have," I told him and signed everything he put in front of me.

I was, and still am, stunned by America's generosity in helping me support my family in foreign land. From that day forward, I became a proud soldier, and I realized how lucky I was to be in such a beautiful country. That magical, patriotic epiphany only grew during my time in the Army when, after a couple promotions, the $100 increased to $200, an amount that even as a civilian working at Tempting Pies wouldn't have been possible.

Meanwhile, in Fort Dix, we were taught discipline and received vigorous physical training. I was growing increasingly excited for the future, and unlike many of the young men who had been drafted, I was looking forward to the opportunity of entering the fray.

One day, we were issued our M1 rifles, and we started training how to use them. Sergeant Slater, in his loud, barky voice, made clear to us that we had to keep them clean and ready at all times.

"When you face the enemy, your rifle and your buddy next to you are the only things you will have to depend on for survival," he told us.

Unlike some of my fellow soldiers, I had held a weapon before. And when I was handed my new rifle, it felt familiar, like welcoming a good friend. Quietly, I longed for the moment when I could finally pull the trigger.

The M1 rifle is a semi-automatic weapon that can fire one round at a time, or it can keep on firing out the whole clip of eight rounds as you keep on pulling the trigger. I remember well the day we marched to a firing range to practice firing our M1s at targets for the first time with live ammunition. Before we took our positions, we were given strict orders, that each one of us, upon command, would fire only one round at a time. Those orders were repeated to ensure that everyone understood. At the target range, I took my position and waited. I was anxious, and when my turn came, I raised my M1 and set my sights at the target that was in the shape of a silhouette of a man, seventy-five yards away. But before I could pull the trigger, something unexpected happen.

Perhaps the demons of my past, which I thought I had exorcised with Kokkinis's death, had somehow returned, and that fateful day of May 1, 1944 flashed before my eyes. To me, the target slowly morphed into Stasinopoulos, my father's killer.

At that moment, I went to a place where there were no orders. Instantly, I unleashed whatever pent-up fury lay within me and fired rapid fire shots until the clip emptied out. The target was completely annihilated. But I wanted more, and before I could reload, Sergeant Slater and a lieutenant named Daniels came over quickly, took my rifle away, and escorted me off the line.

Perhaps on the battlefield, they would have loved me. But at that moment, the US Army was not amused.

Neither were my fellow soldiers, who I could hear snickering off on the sidelines, offering sarcastic comments about how the US Army should "teach them how to speak English first."

I began to worry. I knew I had failed to follow the orders, and I felt that I couldn't bear to be taken away from a place that had felt so right for me. Even though I had lost control of my thoughts at that moment, I knew I belonged in the Army. I think it was because the Army was a place where I could learn to control the chaos that I knew existed inside me. They taught us how to discipline our angry instincts and channel it into something productive. It allowed me to harness what had always been inside me. And now I had failed, and I stood to lose that opportunity.

I was sent back to camp and was charged with insubordination for disobeying orders. Those were very serious charges, and I was facing many years of hard labor and, even worse for me, a dishonorable discharge, which would prevent me from becoming an American citizen.

For a whole week, I was questioned by officers and examined by Army psychiatrists. I was desperate to stay in the Army, so I came up with the best lie that I could and stuck to it: "I had misunderstood the orders."

It was an easy story to sell, considering my broken English. All the while, I knew the truth.

While waiting for my fate, I was ordered to serve as KP, Kitchen Police, a misleading title, which was a punishment supervised by the mess sergeant. It involved scrubbing pots and pans, peeling potatoes, and mopping floors for never-ending hours.

Fortunately, after a couple of weeks of giving the same answers to the same questions, they finally believed that I had misunderstood the orders due to my limited English, and I was allowed to continue with my service.

I was determined after that to finish my training. I worked hard to keep my emotions in check. It wasn't always easy. Occasionally, I would see that flash again, off in the distance, triggering urges to go back to that place of rage that had become so uncomfortably comfortable. I was a man hovering between two worlds at all times. And while it was the Army that had brought me back to that place, I had faith that it was the Army that would help me tame it.

My Army Buddies

CHAPTER 14

Fort Knox— Louisville, Kentucky

After basic training in Fort Dix, I was shipped off to Fort Knox in Kentucky and was assigned to the 3rd Armor Division where another type of training was waiting. Having only been in Uncle George's old Desoto, I now found myself inside Uncle Sam's big tank. At first, I liked the idea of fighting a war from inside the tank, surrounded by six inches of steel. But that thought quickly died when I later learned that a 90 mm shell can go through six inches of steel like a hot knife through butter.

The tank training was much more complicated than the basic training in Fort Dix. And driving a tank was far more complicated than driving my uncle's car. I had gone from shooting an M1 rifle to operating a massive tank and big 90 mm cannon.

But soon, that tank became to me like my loyal steed that ushered me into the future. I trained hard to understand its intricacies and, eventually, I was promoted to Private First Class and given a crew of five rookies to train. My job was to order them to get the tank in shape and ready for an upcoming General's inspection. I had never given an order to anybody before, but quickly, I found myself more comfortable being one of the orderers than one of the ordered. Now, I understood what it was like to be Sergeant Slater, barking orders at strong young men and having them follow you with strict obedience.

Working on the tanks was certainly hard work. It was tough and dirty, and we had to replace every worn-out part of the tank by hand, getting covered in grease and oil under the hot Kentucky sun. These rookies were young and away from home, sort of like me, but they had clearly never experienced the violent trials that had hardened my spirit. And I found myself wanting the best for them. I pushed them when I felt they dragged their feet. I found a sense of paternal pride in my new authority as their leader. There was also a certain degree of glee at my own power that I couldn't deny. I heard them bitching, frequently, about the work, and I wasn't afraid to push back.

"The more you're bitching, the harder work will be," I told them.

I know I was hard on them, but as I reminded them frequently, there is nothing easy in the Army, and in the end, my tough demeanor paid off. During the General's inspection, our tank was awarded as the best and most ready for combat out of every tank in the entire battalion. For our hard work and dedication, we were awarded long weekend passes to the nearby town of Louisville.

I had heard a lot about the Kentucky town from my fellow soldiers who had spent their long weekends there. They spoke of raucous nights at the bars, great music, and mostly, chasing girls. They spent their down time around Fort Knox regaling us with stories of their exploits and yearning to go back.

This would be my first trip there, and I was excited. The word "Louisville" seemed like a fairy tale, a mystical place that only the initiated could visit. Now I felt a degree of wonder that my time had come.

On Saturday morning, I put on my class A uniform and, with my crew of five, boarded a bus to Louisville, which was about twenty-five miles away. Our plan was to hit the town until Sunday night. I felt proud to take my crew with me. I knew they deserved that trip, and I could tell that they had been frustrated with how hard I worked them. But on that bus ride, we smiled, laughed, and joked, and it was the loosest and relaxed I had felt in years.

We got off the bus at the Louisville depot in good spirits, but before entering the building, we saw two huge signs with large arrows pointing to the "white" section and the "black" section of the bus station.

In my short time in America, I had heard some whispers about segregation and the divisive issue of race that was beginning to bubble into the nationwide fight for civil rights. But I had never seen anything so blatant as this.

There was a soldier in our group named Thomas who was black. He was a hard worker, and he had deserved the trip just as much as anyone else on our team. Maybe Thomas had been in these situations before because when he saw the signs, he began to trail off toward the "black" section, turning to us with a wave.

"I'll see you guys back at camp," he said.

I can remember the tone of his voice; it's always stuck with me. In the Army, we were all brothers, I believed. But for him, segregation must have been an inevitable part of everyday life. He said it like a parent says goodbye to their child when they drop them off at school, a quick "have a good day!" It was ordinary, mundane, and routine. Just as surprising to me was how readily the other white rookies waved him off and began moving toward the "white" section.

This was a new situation to me, and it didn't feel right. All I could think about was the same image that had inspired me to embrace the Army: those Allied soldiers coming into our village to save us. That day was, in fact, the first time I had ever seen a black man as there were several in the ranks of those soldiers who liberated us. As a child who had grown up in my sheltered mountain village of farmers, certainly, I noticed the color of their skin, processed our physical differences. But as our parents and neighbors cheered those men, reaching out to touch them as they passed as if they were some prophets from heaven, I saw only heroes, and there was no black or white.

This was a belief that was only reinforced through my training. Every day, we were taught and constantly reminded that we were brothers. We supported one another no matter what, regardless of our nationalities or the color of our skin. It was ingrained in us deeply so that we would act unthinkingly in support of one another. On the battlefield, there was no time for petty differences.

Brotherhood could save our lives. It was the unwritten cardinal rule that underpinned all of our actions.

Although we were off military base, I still believed I was in charge, and I didn't see how our foundational belief of brotherhood should change now that we were in Louisville. I ordered the rookies to stop and caught up with Thomas, stepping in front of him.

"Where are you going? We are together. Why you are leaving us?" I asked him.

"We were together, man, but now look at those signs," he said.

"Those signs are for civilians," I insisted. "They don't apply to us. We are soldiers. We're brothers."

"No, no," Thomas said, waving me off. "You don't understand this at all. I have to go this way. I don't want to cause any trouble to you guys."

Perhaps he too had believed in that simple notion of brotherhood, not the kind that is instilled in the Army, but the grander kind that God intended us to subscribe to, the kind children seem to stumble into, even as adults trample over it. Perhaps he had taken a chance before in the past, believing in that brotherhood, only to be hurt in the end. It was a feeling I could never imagine, to be excluded from the world simply because of the color of your skin. I could see him leaning, uncertain, and could hear his voice insist on following the signs. But soon I felt as sure as ever that he should come with us, as the other four soldiers came over behind me, and we convinced him to come with us.

I didn't know it then, I couldn't possibly know it then, but unfortunately, Thomas was right. I'm certain I never would have realized how dangerous the game we were playing was, especially in a place like Louisville. The racial divide in this city went deeper than I could have possibly imagined, and it was ready to boil over.

It was a only a short time after this incident that an African American family consisting of Andrew Wade, his wife, Charlotte, and their two-year-old daughter, Rosemary, moved into a house in a white neighborhood in Louisville, and the city fell into chaos. The house was shot at and vandalized, and after significant controversy, it was bombed. Fortunately, no one was harmed; however, strangely, they never caught the ones who did it.

It was unthinkable to me that those nice suburban streets with their manicured lawns, and those loving, welcoming American people could be concealing such potent violence. I suppose I had learned it myself as a child, how fear and mistrust can divide a community before you even realize it's bubbling.

We all entered the building together and walked to the coffee shop to have some breakfast. We sat at the counter, waiting for service, but we got nothing but dirty looks from the waitresses who were going back and forth behind the counter.

I noticed that Thomas was getting nervous and very uncomfortable. I took one quick look around and could see that everyone was giving us those same dirty looks. I realized I had made a mistake for not listening to Thomas, and I could feel a sense of danger hanging in the air like a thick fog, and I suddenly felt that, as the leader of this young team, I had a responsibility to keep everyone safe.

As I was trying to think of a way out of this situation, it was confusing to me, to think that here we were, all five of us, trained and ready to be sent out to fight for freedom for a country that we loved, but at that moment, the biggest danger that we faced was at home.

When it became obvious that we wouldn't be served, I told the team that we should leave. But little did I know, a large group of rednecks had started to build up behind us. As we were walking to the door, they moved in to block the exit and jumped on us. But it was Thomas that they wanted, so we circled around him as they hurled fists and insults, calling us terrible racial slurs.

Thanks to the Army, we were well-trained, and we fought them back hard, and during the brawl, I threw a perfect punch that caught one attacker, sending him to the floor with a broken nose that was flowing with blood while another guy was throwing attackers around like rag dolls protecting Thomas. But as hard as we fought, we were outnumbered by at least four to one.

Two military police officers rushed over from their positions at the bus station, but there was little they could do against this angry group that was only getting larger as others were drawn into the mayhem. But the tide finally turned in our favor when another bus from Fort Knox arrived, loaded with soldiers who were looking for a fun time in Louisville.

I had spent a lot of time with soldiers, had heard them complain about the Army, bemoan being drafted. But on that day, I saw the brotherhood that we were taught come to life. When they came off the bus and saw their brothers getting beat up, they didn't waste a second and jumped in to help. They showed off their training that day, and despite the cuts and bruises, I wished it would never end.

It was the Louisville police who ultimately broke up the violence, but the fight didn't end there. The officers believed that Thomas and our team were the guilty party because we had not obeyed the signs despite the fact that the rednecks had thrown the first punches. Those people were let go, and they moved to arrest us, starting with Thomas, who now took quick glances at us, a face that screamed for help, with a hint of "I told you so."

Fortunately, at the same time, another bus filled with military police had arrived, headed by a real tough captain who liked to shout first and ask questions later. He saw us beaten up and bruised and arrested; he didn't hesitate. He got into the face of the police captain, demanding that we be released.

"Those are my boys, and I am taking them home," he said. "Now get out of my way."

After a short standoff, we were put on a bus back to camp where a colonel confronted us. He wasn't happy with our behavior, and he yelled at us profusely for getting tangled into a terrible situation. But he ended on a positive note, praising our commitment to one another and our bravery. It left us confused but satisfied.

I still struggle to understand how a Greek immigrant who was not yet an American citizen could have more rights to a cup of coffee than a soldier who was born in this country.

It was the last time that anything like that happened between the Fort Knox soldiers and the people of Louisville again. I suppose it had to do with the Army's threat to city leaders that they'd put Louisville off limits to soldiers, a move that would undoubtedly halt the flow of revenue generated from visiting soldiers, a major source of income.

But the city continued the segregation against its own citizens. It was a shameful period. Even the great Muhammad Ali, born Cassius Clay in Louisville, returned home from the Olympics with a gold medal in tow, only to be refused service in a restaurant. In frustration, he famously threw the medal into the Ohio River. Many years later, as destiny would have it, Ali and I would exchange our stories, but he never held a grudge.

I spent eighteen months in Kentucky, and I came to love it. Outside of its racism, there was a lot to like in Kentucky: its bluegrass, its fast horses, and country music. I got to love it for its bourbon and fast women.

Country music and bluegrass was just about the only music to be heard in Kentucky, and I grew to like it well. The guitar and banjo reminded me of the sounds of the Greek bouzouki and mandolin. That was until one day, I was listening to the radio and something different came on. It was a song called "South of the Border." Its blaring horns at the intro immediately entranced me. Then it was the voice, that voice that boomed with a cool nonchalance, as strong as a thunderstorm and as smooth as Jack Daniels. I tapped my foot along with a dumb smile on my face.

"The mission bells told me—ding dong—that I mustn't stay, south of the border down Mexico way."

I wanted to know who the singer was, and when the song ended, the announcer said it was Frank Sinatra. That was the day that I became a fan of Sinatra, and in the following years, I kept listening to the radio, anxiously hoping to hear his songs. Little did I know then that years later I would meet Frank and create a long-lasting friendship of more than three decades—one that inspired me to write a book.

CHAPTER 15

Derailed

Soon, I learned that a veteran soldier could put in a request for transfer to an overseas base. Many saw this is an opportunity to travel free and see the world, but with the war going on, others saw it as a risk because getting assigned to Korea could put you in the thick of combat.

For me, it was a risk worth taking. I put in a request to go overseas, hoping I would get transferred to Germany. That way, I could get a few days free and travel the short distance to visit my family in Greece. I knew it was a long shot, but deep inside, I longed to return home for just a moment, knowing that once I was out of the Army, I'd have very few opportunities to travel back to Greece on my own.

Even more, there was always that image in my head that never quite left me—of those Allied soldiers entering our village, that heroic swagger that they carried themselves with, the cheers and the thanks. Nothing would make me prouder than to enter my village clad in the same uniform. It was a dream I couldn't shake. But it was often interrupted by an unwelcome thought: *What if I'm sent to Korea?*

And each time, I landed on the same answer: *So let it be.*

Waiting for my orders to be shipped overseas, the days and weeks passed slowly until one day, Lieutenant Daniels gave me an order to report to the battalion commander, Colonel Stufflebeem, at the headquarters for a special assignment.

I had a deep feeling that this was a result of my request for overseas transfer, and I was eager to see the colonel, hoping I would be sent to Germany. I felt as if I were floating with each step I took toward the headquarters. When I entered the building, a sergeant at the entrance escorted me to the colonel's office.

"Private First Class Pavlopoulos, reporting as ordered, sir," I said with a sharp salute.

The colonel returned the salute and waved me closer to a long table where a collection of drawings and plans were scattered. Then, he circled a remote area on a large map hanging on the wall. When I saw the circle on the map, I immediately felt that this special assignment could only mean one thing, and I was sure of it.

This is it, I told myself. *I'm going to Korea.*

But I was wrong.

"This area here is designated for a Little League Babe Ruth baseball field for Fort Knox," the colonel said in a commanding voice. "You have shown good leadership, and I am promoting you to Specialist First Class to be in charge of the rookies we're assigning to the detail."

Immediately, my imagination ran wild. I was bewildered. All of my plans to see my family, to take a proud walk through my village in my uniform, to possibly fight in Korea, at that moment—all gone. And now I was involved in something new, baseball, which I had never heard of before in Greece. For a few seconds, my instinct was to try to piece together what role this could possibly play for the war effort. I came up empty.

By now, I had learned two very important things about life in the Army: never volunteer for anything, and never try to get out of any detail that an officer is assigning you to. Because if you volunteer, you'll be stuck with grunt work. Like the day I remember a field sergeant asking for volunteers to do "paperwork." The whole platoon raised our hands, hoping to be inside a cool office and out of tough training in the hot Kentucky sun. Instead, we were all duped into cleaning up papers and trash that had littered Fort Knox after a strong bout of wind. Meanwhile, if you try to get out of an assignment, you'll usually be successful, only to be assigned to something worse, like cleaning up the grease pits in the kitchen.

So as per my unofficial training in the unwritten rules of Army life, I held my tongue. The colonel gave me a pair of new stripes and told me to report to Lieutenant Daniels for the details.

"Yes, sir," I said. I saluted the colonel and left his office, and on my way to see Lieutenant Daniels, I had one big concern: What the hell was baseball?

In my short time in America, certainly, I had heard some of the guys talk about a game called baseball, had seen people watching games on their black-and-white TVs, but had never paid any attention and knew nothing about America's national pastime. I didn't know what a baseball field was, let alone how to build one, and a new kind of fear settled in.

I had seen war, had seen killings, and had been in life-and-death situations. Sure, I was scared. But basic instincts had taken control, and I had simply reacted, and I lived in that world for so long that fear became my new normal. Truthfully, adapting to the complex intricacies of average American life had always frightened me a good deal more, from buying the *New York Times* for my uncle to driving through the Lincoln tunnel. And now, I realized how woefully unsuited I was for this task. I felt I had been thrown to the deep end of the lake and didn't know how to swim.

I was told by Lieutenant Daniels that I would have twenty-five rookie soldiers under my command doing manual work, and my job was to make sure they were doing their jobs correctly. I was good at giving orders, but how the hell was I going to give orders that I didn't understand myself?

My mind was searching for answers of how to handle this strange task. But I couldn't find any, and out of desperation, I was thinking of spilling it all out and telling the lieutenant that I was not the right person for the job. But then the thought that I was surrounded by a bunch of all-American young men who knew all about baseball since childhood gave me hope and courage like a guiding star. I realized that most of them had even played the game themselves, and most importantly, they knew all about the baseball field. With that thought, I decided that I would rely on those rookies to do all of the thinking and work.

So out of desperation, that's exactly what I did. And boy, was I on the money.

Those guys knew everything about baseball, including how the field should look. And from day one, I let them do all the thinking for me. I quickly discovered that, in the Army, it's the stripes that do all the talking, and the colonel knew that.

And me? I faked my way through the entire project by walking around, looking at everyone with a critical eye as if I knew what I was looking for. And to make sure they knew I was around, I would approach a group working on something and ask them, "Do you know what you are doing here, soldiers?"

Thinking I was testing them and fearing my authority, they would respond, explaining everything to me.

"Very well, soldiers," I'd say. "Carry on."

Then I'd walk away quickly before anyone could ask me any questions.

By watching them work and listening to their answers, I was able to piece together the mechanics of a baseball field though I knew nothing about the game itself. I've always been grateful to those guys for making me look good when I couldn't do that myself. And even though I tried to do my best to look serious and tough, I gave them many breaks, making sure they had plenty of food and refreshments. I'm sure that they saw me and believed me to be a tough superior who was testing them. But inside, I felt like a student, bringing an apple to the teacher.

Finally, one day, the field was completed. I saw my first baseball game at that field, its inaugural game. I sat with the colonel and all the top brass and, not knowing much about the game, I clapped when they clapped, cheered when they cheered. Once, I got strange looks when I started clapping at a time I shouldn't have. But otherwise it turned out to be a happy day.

The colonel was pleased with the field and so happy that he had given me my assignment. A few days later, he issued to me a letter of appreciation and gave me a new assignment as his personal driver, another task I was woefully unsuited for.

Besides my uncle's few lessons on how to drive his old Desoto, where I had difficulties shifting gears, I had no other driving experience. I had to spend days at the motor pool taking lessons before I reported to my new assignment.

I never would make it to Germany, Greece, or Korea during my service. But in my time in the Army, I learned the value of teamwork and brotherhood. I also discovered baseball. That sport, along with music, became my favorite part of American culture, I think because, in many ways, it taught me the same lessons that the Army did.

It's a beautiful game, baseball. Each inning is a pocket of anticipation, a story that can twist suddenly and violently with one swing, one pitch. It's a game that prides the individual, placing them in the spotlight of the batter's box without losing the significance of teamwork. It reminded me of Fort Knox and my service, that sense of brotherhood, that sense that if you wear the uniform, you're part of a team, and when it's your turn in the lineup or in the fox hole, you better be damn sure you can pick your brothers up.

Years later, I would tell the story of that little baseball field in Fort Knox to a man who knew more about that sport than many come to learn in a lifetime—one who would become one of my best and dearest friends: George Steinbrenner. One night, we were eating cheeseburgers at P.J. Clarke's in New York. At that point in my life, my time in the Army would feel like another lifetime completely. To think that I didn't know what baseball was would seem like a ridiculous notion, especially sitting next to the owner of the New York Yankees.

"That's how life is," George told me. "When I was plucking chickens at my father's chicken farm in Cleveland, I didn't know I'd one day be the owner of the Yankees."

DINO PAVLOU

PFC US Army Fort Knox

HEADQUARTERS COMBAT COMMAND "A"
3D ARMORED DIVISION (Spearhead)
Fort Knox, Kentucky

AIBAK-A   3 December 1954

SUBJECT: Letter of Appreciation

TO: Private Constantine Pavlopupoulas, US51313805
        Company B, 7th Medium Tank Battalion
        Combat Command "A"
        3d Armored Division (Spearhead)
        Fort Knox, Kentucky

     I am pleased to note that on 30 November 1954 your tank was inspected
by the G-4, 3d Armored Division Inspection Team and received no deficiencies
either for the Tank Artillery Inspection or the Combat Vehicular Inspection.

     The fact that your equipment has been maintained in such a superior
state indicates that you have not only absorbed your training and have a
superior knowledge of Tank Maintenance but also take pride in your equipment and your job. I am most happy to have you serve under my command
and am sure that your performance of duty will continue to make you worthy
of the name "Tanker."

                              H. M. FONDREN
                              Colonel, Armor
                              Commanding

US Army Letter of Appreciation

CHAPTER 16

My First Encounter

Driving for the colonel was a detail that every soldier in Fort Knox wanted to have. No more Sergeant Slaters, no more hard training, no more inspections, no more standing in lines. And most importantly, I had every weekend off, and I spent them all in Louisville, hanging out in roadside bars and dance halls, enjoying Kentucky's bourbon and friendly girls.

Back at the camp, my daily work was the easiest in the whole United States Army—I was basically doing nothing. Every morning, at 6:00 a.m., I would get up, take a shower and shave, and then put on my class-A uniform, and while skipping all the lines, the morning inspections, and marches, I would go straight to the mess hall for breakfast. Then I would pick up the colonel's Jeep from the motor pool, already gassed up, buffed, and shined by the rookies, and I would drive a short distance to the colonel's office and be there by 8:00 a.m. There, I'd park in front and wait until the colonel had to be driven somewhere.

Other than driving the colonel out to the fields sometimes to inspect the troops, there wasn't much else to do. But I had to keep the Jeep ready for him, and sometimes I'd become easily bored, hoping that the colonel would come out so that I could drive somewhere, anywhere, to get me out of my boredom. On the other hand, I would rather be bored than grinding away at the daily grueling tasks of military life.

When I first became the colonel's driver, I was told that, if I was driving the Jeep and the colonel wasn't in it, then the colonel's shield, mounted on the front of the jeep, must be covered. But one morning, I picked up the Jeep, and as I was driving to the colonel's office, I noticed that every soldier was saluting me. I quickly realized that I had forgotten to cover the shield, but I liked the attention and kept driving with a big grin on my face. It was like a practical joke that only I would enjoy. I decided to swing by my old barracks, just at the time when my former drill sergeant was drilling a platoon, and I slowed down, almost to a stop just so I could see the sergeant saluting.

I laughed to myself. It was a fun distraction for me. Some days grew more boring than others, and I needed to find ways to pass my time. But that decision didn't sit well with the sergeant, and he reported me to headquarters. I probably should have lost my position, but for some reason, the colonel let me off easy, issuing a warning: "Keep the shield covered," he said.

So that was mostly the extent of the excitement that my new job offered—until one day when I got all the excitement I could handle.

The colonel rushed out of his office all excited and quickly jumped into the Jeep. I had never seen him like that before; he was usually a very stoic man, and for a moment, I thought another war had started.

"Drive to the airport," he ordered.

"Yes, sir," I said and quickly started the Jeep and took off.

"Should I turn on the siren, sir?"

"No, that's not necessary. There is plenty of time," he said. And in a few minutes into the drive, he had calmed down some, but soon, as if he couldn't hold back his excitement, he wanted to talk.

"We are meeting a very important military man who is coming to visit Fort Knox," he said, all excited. "His name is Audie Murphy. Sound familiar to you?"

Familiar?

That was an understatement, and when I heard we were meeting Audie Murphy, I felt as if a 90 mm shell exploded on the hood of the Jeep and I almost drove it into a ditch. Although I had never met this man, his reputation preceded him. He was the greatest American hero of World War II, the most decorated soldier of the United States; he had become an established movie star and a household name.

He was considered the "Babe Ruth of War."

Driving to the airport, my mind was awhirl with excitement. Only a few weeks earlier, I had seen the movie *To Hell and Back*, the story of Murphy's military life, in which he played himself. Although I had seen him in the movie, still, I envisioned him as an impressive, tall man, like other big movie stars at the time like John Wayne or Anthony Quinn and Gregory Peck. I expected him to tower over the rest of us and his voice to be strong and deep.

But to my surprise, none of this was true. The man who got out of the plane and walked over to us was small and nimble with a round baby face. When he spoke, his voice was quiet and calm. I snapped to attention and offered a salute, which he sharply returned, but all that time I couldn't stop thinking he was just a kid.

That impression died quickly. For underneath those boyish features were scars of war. In one battle in France, he famously ordered his unit to withdraw from certain slaughter to safer grounds, and all alone, he climbed on top of a burning tank and used its .50 caliber machine gun to kill more than two hundred Nazi soldiers and save his unit.

Vast experiences were evident upon his face for anyone who looked closely. His eyes were sharp and intent, and underneath that soft voice was an intensity that grabbed your attention. He instilled respect simply by being next to you.

When I shook his hand, I was taken by an overwhelming and incredible, inexplicable sensation that I have only known three times in my life. I suppose it was due to being in the presence of greatness. The first time I felt it was that day with Audie Murphy, but I was destined to feel the same sensation twice more later: once when I first met with Frank Sinatra, and lastly meeting Buzz Aldrin, one of the two men who first walked on the moon.

Although by then, Murphy had risen to a new fame as a high-caliber movie star in Western movies, in his heart he always remained a soldier and had come to Fort Knox for a visit as he often visited other army camps. I was assigned to drive him and the colonel around, and during that time, I noticed that Murphy much preferred to spend his time with the plain soldiers than with the military brass. He enjoyed eating with them at the mess hall rather than with the officers in their dining rooms. I clearly understood he was a soldier's soldier.

During the couple days that I spent with him, that feeling of greatness never really left, but I grew increasingly comfortable around him. He was very sociable with a modest personality that made me feel like I was driving around a plain ordinary Joe instead of a stiff, high-ranking military officer, or an egotistical megastar.

He noticed my name, Pavlopoulos, pasted on my jacket, and because of my heavy accent, he asked me where I was born. And when I told him I was from Greece, Murphy enthusiastically started telling me his welcoming experiences in his short time passing through Greece on his way to Italy during the war. He told me some war stories there, and I shared with him some of my own experiences, and before his visit was over, we had struck up a good friendship. When I drove him back to the airport, and before we said goodbye, he must have read my mind. He wrote a number on a piece of paper and gave it to me.

"If you ever get to California, this is where you can reach me," he said.

One day, I would take him up on his offer. And that's a story for another chapter.

Audie Murphy in the Army

CHAPTER 17

A New Start

After serving more than two years in the Army, I got my discharge and left with a heart full of pride and a head full of life lessons. I never did go overseas but felt like I had learned more about the world than I ever could have expected.

I returned to my uncle George's house in Elizabeth, and for the first time, I met my other cousin Costas, who had been discharged before me and was now pursuing his profession as pharmacist. This house was now a much happier place than the one I had left. Now it felt as if a heavy weight had been lifted from Uncle George and Aunt Eleni. I no longer caught them sitting in silence, lost in thought and worry, their minds turned to Korea. They were thrilled to have their son and nephew back home.

I had followed my uncle's advice and learned English, so I no longer needed my little brat cousin Kimon as an interpreter. I was stronger, more mature, and more confident, and I wanted a job where I could earn more than seventy-five cents an hour. While I had no education or skills, I knew that my two years serving in the Army were well spent and made me feel like a college graduate. I had become an American citizen; I felt energized, disciplined, more mature and wiser. I better understood my place in the wonderful melting pot of America, and I felt like I was ready for a new start.

There were some job opportunities in New Jersey, but I felt in my heart that I was being called to something greater. And ever since I had arrived in America as a foreign seventeen-year-old kid, the image of the New York skyline from the deck of the *Italia* was imprinted on my memory. From New Jersey I could see that vast jungle of skyscrapers, and I felt something calling me, challenging me, like sirens singing from off in the distance. As a newly arrived immigrant kid, that city seemed intimidating. But now, it felt like a world of promise.

"It's now or never," I told myself.

I always valued my uncle George's advice, and besides, I didn't want to move to New York without at least telling him. When I told him, he was hesitant at first, but then, I think he realized that my hope to leave meant he had succeeded as my sponsor; he had done a good job in helping me find a home in America, and now, I was ready to go out on my own. With a smile, he suggested that I consider Astoria, a suburb of Manhattan with a strong Greek community.

The next morning, I stuffed my army duffle bag with what few belongings I had. I thanked my uncle and aunt for everything they had done for me. I said goodbye to Costas and to little Kimon, who, to my surprise, seemed sad to see me go, and I set off to catch the next bus to New York City.

The bus took me to Forty-First Street and Eighth Avenue. I had never been to the heart of Manhattan, and I took my time exploring, strolling around Forty-Second Street and Broadway, admiring the beauty of Times Square with all its theaters and glittering lights, the streams of people and cars that rushed like rivers to the sea. I had never seen anything like it. For me, it was breathtaking, and right away I felt like I was home.

First, I had to find a job. I had very little money and had no place to stay. I carried the duffle bag with everything I owned strapped over my shoulder, and even for a young army man like myself, it was beginning to get heavy. I followed my uncle's advice, and in the afternoon, I took a fifteen-minute train ride to Astoria. As the train entered a dark tunnel and took some sharp turn, swaying me around a bit, it reminded me of my frightening experience at sea, and suddenly I thought of my friend, Elias, and I wondered if he too had settled in Astoria.

The train came rocketing out of the tunnel, and I was fascinated when I realized that it was now traveling on elevated tracks. Below us, I could see the houses, scrunched together, roofs outfitted with those television antennas that had once seemed so strange. I smiled to myself; I now knew what those things were. But still, I was quietly flabbergasted thinking of that dark tunnel that we had emerged from, and how, only a few minutes ago, we were speeding under the deep waters of the East River and now, somehow, were traveling over Astoria's rooftops.

After many stops, the train finally made its last stop on Thirty-First Street near Ditmars Boulevard where I got off and spent some time strolling around, once again with my big bag on my shoulder, and I found a comfortable peace in the Greek storefronts and Greek people. It was like a tinier, more crowded version of my village, and I loved the excitement and energy. Something was telling me that, eventually, Astoria would be my next home.

By late afternoon I was getting hungry, and I wanted to find a Greek restaurant where I could sit down and eat my first Greek meal in years. I passed a vegetable store and asked the owner for a recommendation, and he told me to go to the "Zapeon Pavillion" at the end of Steinway Street, one of Astoria's biggest corridors.

After a long walk, I arrived. It had a large outdoor garden with tall trees that shielded it from the sun, and it was filled with tables and chairs, mostly occupied with elder people, sipping on their wine or coffee, talking loudly and smoking their cigarettes. It seemed to be a gathering place of friends, where one could spend hours that felt like minutes.

When I walked in with my duffle bag hanging on my shoulder, I noticed all eyes turned on me as I took a table. I guess it was something new to them seeing a young Greek man in an American Army uniform, and right away, some came over with smiling faces and jumped straight into pleasant conversation, mostly wanting to know my name and what part of Greece I was from.

But suddenly, all the attention I was receiving was sucked away, and everyone turned toward a police captain who had just entered the restaurant. He was a man in his early forties with a sharp police uniform that attracted attention and demanded respect. He was friendly, and I heard him talking to everyone fluently in Greek. Like all those around me who were surprised to see a Greek-American soldier, I was just as surprised also to see a Greek police captain. During their friendly conversations, he must have noticed that I was new, and he approached me to welcome me with a hearty handshake. After we exchanged some pleasantries, he asked me where I came from.

"From Fort Knox, Kentucky," I told him. "I am visiting here, and I am also looking for a job."

I imagined myself for a moment wearing a police uniform. It would be the ideal job for me, and I hoped that he would take my comment as a job application.

"What kind of a job? What can you do?" he asked.

"Besides shooting guns, I have no other skills," I told him.

"That is a skill," he said with a smile.

To my surprise, he then introduced himself as John Poulos, Father John Poulos. He was a priest who was also an honorary police captain of the local precinct, a title that he had earned for his service to the community. I was told later that he was basically the mayor of Astoria. He was a powerful and influential voice who commanded respect, or fear, from the local politicians, who would do anything for the community that Father Poulos asked.

With an upbeat tone in his voice, he asked me to meet him the next day at his office at the Saint Demetrios Church.

"I will find a job for you," he said, as if it were as simple as picking fruit from a tree.

I found comfort in his voice and found myself happier, lighter even, like a nagging responsibility that had been hanging over my head had dissipated. I treated myself to a delicious lamb dinner and some Greek wine, and later, I asked my new friends at the place if there was a hotel nearby where I could spend the night.

That was a mistake.

"The best hotels in Astoria are our homes," someone said, and the rest of them agreed.

"You are welcome to stay in my house," one offered, and quickly another made the same offer, and soon others jumped in and started welcoming me into their homes. And soon it turned into an argument, and I had very little say. I appreciated their hospitality, however. A man named Theodore Skaris finally won the argument. He was a husky man in his fifties with a scratchy voice, the type that wouldn't take no for an answer. He was so persistent that he even paid for my dinner.

Theodore later explained to me why the people there had been so quick to offer me a home. Every one of those men had emigrated from Greece and had left their families behind before the war. They were all like my Uncles Dimitri and George, and they were thankful to the Allies and to America and her soldiers for ending the civil war and sending so much help to their country.

After a night of excitement, drinking and new friends, Theodore took me to his house. It was a small house on Forty-Second Street and Thirty-Sixth Avenue in Astoria that was also home to his wife and two daughters, Maria and Vasso. They made me feel as if I was their own.

I woke up early the next morning and walked to the Saint Demetrios Church about three blocks away and met with Father Poulos. After a short conversation, he dialed a number and I heard him talking to someone on the other end named Jimmy.

"Jimmy, this is Father Poulos," he said. "I am sending a young man to see you. He just got out of the Army, and I want you to give him a good job at your place."

His voice didn't sound like he was asking for a favor. It was more like he was giving an order. But it wasn't an order like those given in the Army, forceful and demanding. It was slick, like he was simply convincing Jimmy that he wanted this too.

"That's very good, Jimmy. I knew I could count on you," Father Poulos said. "I'll see you in church Sunday."

He wrote on a piece of paper an address in Manhattan and told me to go there and find his friend Jimmy.

I left Father Poulos, anxious to find Jimmy and land a job. On the way, I wondered what kind of job it might be, what kind of money I might be making. But I trusted Father Poulos. He seemed to carry a wisdom that most couldn't amass in a lifetime. It never crossed my mind that on that day, I was about to begin a decade's long career that would change my life forever.

CHAPTER 18

Mabel Mercer's By-Line Room

Carrying my duffle bag, I arrived at East Fifty-Sixth Street, just off Fifth Avenue, and I stopped outside to read the marquee of an odd little place that looked like a bar. It read: "Mabel Mercer's By-Line Room."

It was early in the afternoon, and when I entered, the place was empty, except for one man in his mid-fifties, short and bald and wearing a short white waiter's jacket. When he saw me, he waved me over and introduced himself as Jimmy.

"I am the head waiter and the Union Delegate here," he told me. "Father Poulos told me you are looking for a job, and so let me show you around."

The place was small, but by its plush decor, I could tell it was a ritzy, upscale sort of night club that I had never seen before. I could imagine rich men in suits and dazzling women in fur and diamonds sitting in the cushy chairs. For me, who had spent the last two years in the Kentucky hills, sleeping in an army barracks, and drinking in roadside bars in Louisville, it was intimidating. And I couldn't quite imagine myself feeling comfortable in such a place, not yet anyway.

I was anxious to find a job, work hard, and make good money, but Jimmy never mentioned anything about money. This guy was such a fast talker, and he gave me no chance to ask my own questions. He was showing me where everything was, speedily talking to me about the art of serving, and acting like I had already taken the job. When we got to the kitchen, I felt like I was back in the Army working K.P. again, waiting for my time to come, to get my discharge and move on. And so, right then, I made my decision.

"Thank you, Jimmy," I told him. "But this is not for me. I never did this before, and I have no experience."

But Jimmy had strict orders from Father Poulos.

"You'll learn just like I did," he insisted, sure of himself. "I'll be helping you until you learn. It's a hard night's work. But you'll be making good money here, like $80 to $100 a night."

My eyes widened. I wanted to make good money, but eighty to hundred dollars a night, at that time, was a week's pay for people with skills and education. Now, I could see dollar signs all over, and I quickly pushed away all of my self-doubts.

"What the hell," I told myself. "If I could build a baseball field, I can do this easily."

I took the job, and on my first night, I was surprised to see how the place got filled up so quickly, and I soon felt lost. I could do nothing but follow Jimmy around like a shadow, watching his every move and trying my best to learn. He was doing all the work, taking the orders, and serving.

It was a strange atmosphere; the work was busy and systematic like the inside of a beehive, with waiters buzzing by left and right. They were like the cogs of a quietly humming machine, working to keep the customers happy without getting in anyone's way, and I was doing my best to keep up, following Jimmy and learning until, suddenly, everything stood still. The talking stopped, the laughter stopped, and the buzzing waiters stopped. All heads turned toward the stage, and everyone began applauding for a black lady who had walked into the light.

She was kind of heavy-set with a friendly smile, and she walked elegantly with an air of royalty. She sat upright on a chair in front of the piano where a pianist was treading his fingers lightly over the ivory keys, spilling a tinkle of notes. She draped a handkerchief over her hand, waiting for the applause to subside.

I looked to Jimmy, a little confused, and before I could even ask him, he explained. "That's Mabel Mercer, the singer," he said. "And we don't serve while she sings."

I followed him to the back of the room in the dark shadows where we joined the other waiters away from view.

I was used to Kentucky country music, electric guitars, and banjos, and when Mabel started to sing, I at first couldn't understand why all these people had come in bunches to listen. She didn't have a strong voice, she had no band behind her aside from the soft piano music, and she sang with no microphone. She was certainly not like other singers I had heard. Yet as I looked at the crowd, I saw only smiles, eyes riveted, faces of wonder, enjoying the moment.

The more I listened, the more fascinated I became, and the more I started to understand the magic of Mabel Mercer. Perhaps it was the happy faces of the people in the crowd, but soon I realized I was watching something special. Mabel's voice politely commanded attention. With her British accent glinting off each syllable, she clearly separated every word, dividing each phrase into clear, delightful morsels; listening to her was the same as enjoying a savory sweet dessert. If country music was like a hot Kentucky barbecue, Mabel's voice was like a rich chocolate mousse. She was a poet reciting a musical poem, and even without a microphone, Mabel's clear voice could be heard and understood from every corner of the room. And the more she sang, the more she was capturing my attention. Nothing would tear me, or the audience, away. Little did I know that Mabel had also captured the attention of some of the most famous singers of the era.

On any given night there was someone famous sitting within the crowd; they were mostly upcoming singers at the time, the likes of a young Johnny Mathis, Nat King Cole, Julie Andrews, Sammy Davis Jr., and an Astoria guy named Tony Bennett, and countless others who saw Mabel as their mentor, and they came to listen and learn. For those singers, the By-Line Room was like a church of music. And Mabel Mercer was the pastor.

But it was Frank Sinatra who was her most loyal disciple. He never missed a night when he was in town. He loved Mabel's singing style and adored her personality. He dubbed her the "Lady of Song" and the "Singer's Singer." Sinatra would stay all night, and Mabel would sit and chat with him in between her shows.

That was exciting for me. I had been a fan of Sinatra ever since I heard his song "South of the Border" on the radio in Fort Knox.

"The Mission bells told me—Ding Dong—that I mustn't stay south of the border down Mexico way."

Since that time, I had listened to much of his music, seen his movies, read about him in the papers, but I never imagined that in only a few years, we both be in the same room, talking to each other. The first time I got to serve him was after I had been working at the By-Line Room for several weeks. He was with Ava Gardner, still his wife at that time. I was a little nervous, but by then I was more competent as a waiter and I had become more confident approaching the mega stars.

"Good evening, Mr. and Mrs. Sinatra." They both returned the greeting, and Frank, looking at me, quickly realized that I was new at the place.

"What is your name, pal?" he asked with interest.

"Dino, sir," I said.

He noted it quietly to himself and proceeded to order their drinks. Other times, I had heard him calling Jimmy and the other waiters by their first names, and it was clear to me then that he knew everybody's name, and now I was glad he also knew mine. Later, I discovered that Sinatra never liked to call anyone "waiter" or "bus boy" or "bartender." To him, every working person was exactly that: a person. And to Frank, every person has a name worth knowing.

I was glad to know that he saw me that way. But I could never have imagined that, one day, I'd get to call him "friend," and that our longtime companionship had started right there, with me calling him "sir" and him, unexpectedly, calling me "Dino."

Frank Sinatra

CHAPTER 19

The Last Word

Working at Mabel Mercer's By-Line Room, I was immersed in a fascinating environment, like a mini ecosystem hidden in New York City. Mabel's regular crowd was a hodgepodge of interesting people, all with their own stories and personalities and relationships, and I came to know most of them. And then there were all the celebrities. I felt like I had been granted access to a secret, exclusive world, brushing shoulders with some very well-known people in the entertainment world.

And then there was Mabel Mercer, the reason they all came and the center of the universe inside that little nightclub ecosystem. She was a wonderful, kind, and sweet lady, with the air of a gracious host, welcoming everyone as if the By-Line Room was her home and we were her houseguests.

In the meantime, I made the wise decision to take advantage of free education that was sponsored by the GI Bill, and I had enrolled in a school for radio, television, and electronics. But after I worked at the By-Line Room for a while, I started hearing those mission bells telling me that I should stay, and so I eventually dropped out of school. I was lucky. For me, it worked out. But dropping out of a free school is generally a bad idea.

As great as the job was and as wonderful as the people around me were, there were others there who cared little about the family atmosphere that we had created. That included one of my bosses, Mabel's partner, Eddie, a hard-nosed, tough talking New Yorker, focused strictly on business and numbers. And while I would occasionally see tremors of discord bubbling behind closed doors, I didn't suspect that a full-on earthquake was coming. I would be content as long as I was making good money. But Eddie and another guy, a silent partner and attorney named Alex Lenes, were quietly unhappy with Mabel. And as time went on, it became increasingly common to hear heated arguments coming out of their small office in the back next to the kitchen. It was all about money; Eddie was pressuring Mabel to allow service to continue while she performed. He claimed they were losing money because Mabel sang without a microphone in a low voice and didn't want the waiters serving while she was performing, fearing they would interfere with her singing.

"Use a microphone so the customers can hear you," they insisted.

For them, money was their first priority. But for Mabel, it was something else. She loved her fans, and she had built that family of supporters doing what she did best: playing in a quiet, mellow atmosphere, letting her followers soak in those special moments.

"My fans come here because they like my style and the way that I sing," she'd say. "I won't change anything."

Being a professional, she would end the conversation by leaving Eddie and Alex behind, putting on her usual smile and getting on stage with her happy flair, always ready to please her devoted and waiting crowd. However, those heated arguments continued on with more intensity, and it had slowly become clear that we were on the verge of a major shift. That happened when, one Monday night, instead of Mabel taking the stage, it was a singer named Buddy Greco, a well-known piano singer with a band behind him. They filled the room with a good but louder sound.

Buddy also had a good following, but it was different from Mabel's crowd. They were chattier and heavier drinkers, and they kept us waiters busy even as Buddy was singing. Meanwhile, Eddie would roam around with a big smile on his face, one that I never knew he had. It didn't take long for the By-Line Room to lose its mellow atmosphere. Mabel's fans and the celebrities would come, too, but after a while, they started to take their business elsewhere. It wasn't because of Buddy's singing; it was Mabel they wanted.

One night, Frank Sinatra came in with his entourage, expecting to see Mabel. He knew and he liked Buddy Greco, and they spoke for a while. But then, Frank went to speak with Eddie, wanting to know what happened to Mabel. I heard Eddie tell him that Mabel needed some rest and that she would return in a few weeks. Perhaps Sinatra was concerned about Mabel's health, or maybe he had caught wind of the feud that had been bubbling for some time, but he stood there in front of Eddie, and I heard him ask when Mabel was coming back. And when he didn't get the answers he wanted, he turned around and left abruptly.

But as the great Yogi Berra would say, "It's not over 'til it's over."

Four weeks passed and there was no sign of Mabel's return, and Buddy was still the entertainer. One evening, when I came in to work, I noticed that the marquee out front had been changed from "Mabel Mercer's By-Line Room" to the "By-Line Room." I knew then that Eddie had lied to Sinatra and that Mabel would not be returning in a few weeks, as he had said.

Unlike Mabel, Eddie had more of an ego and a bad attitude. He was easily angered and rude toward the staff. And with Mabel gone now, Eddie roamed the place more freely, talking to the guests during Buddy's performances and ordering us around. Some of us were grumbling about leaving instead of putting up with Eddie's nonsense. This was a small place, we were only five waiters, and we had a rotation system where each night, one of us would be the "closing man," having to stay late to clean up the tables after all the customers were gone while Eddie would be in the office counting the night's receipts.

There was one night when I was the closing man. It was around 3:30 a.m. The place had emptied out, and I was picking up empty glasses off the tables. It was just me, Eddie in his office, and a porter named Jose who was cleaning up the kitchen. Suddenly, the door swung open and Frank Sinatra walked in, alone and all fired up.

"Dino, where is Eddie?" he asked as he stormed past me.

Before I could answer, he was in Eddie's office, leaving the door open behind him, and I could hear and see everything.

"What have you done to Mabel?" I heard him scream, his voice full of anger. "You threw her out of her own place?"

Eddie stammered for a moment, but before he could say anything, Sinatra continued, "Go ahead, you big liar, lie to me again and tell me that she needs rest. Is that why you took her name off the marquee?"

Eddie tried to calm things down. "You know, Frankie, it's a fickle business and we need to make changes, something that appeals to today's customers," he said.

But Sinatra wouldn't have it.

"Now listen to me, you slimy bastard," he said, appearing ready to pounce on Eddie. "This is Mabel's home. She made it. People didn't come here to see you. They came here to see Mabel. Bring her back."

That's when Eddie was pushed one step too far, and the next thing he said was a grave mistake.

"Look, Frank, I don't tell you how to sing. Don't tell me how to run my club."

And that did it. Frank grabbed Eddie by the collar and brought their faces close together. "Your club?" he hissed. "You're a worthless bum who couldn't bring two flies into this joint. Mabel built this club. And now you're kicking her out. You're nothing but a lowlife bum."

He let Eddie's collar go in disgust and started toward the door.

Eddie was a large man. He could have fought back, or at least made an effort to defend himself, but instead, he just brushed himself off and sat in his chair looking defeated, staring at Sinatra as he walked out.

I was standing there, a little amused, and glad to see that someone stood up to Eddie. And as Sinatra passed by me, still fired up, he shot me a quick look. But then, like he remembered something else, he turned around to go after Eddie again.

I wanted to see Eddie sweat again, but I knew Jose was in the kitchen and could hear everything. I wanted Sinatra to know that, so I stepped in front of him and, in a low voice, told him that there was a porter in the kitchen, and he could hear everything from there.

I think he understood that I was on his side and he gave me another, different kind of look and without a word, he walked out.

After that, there was no word spoken between me and Eddie or Jose. We finished our work for the night, Eddie locked up the place, we said good night, and we went our separate ways.

I took the subway back to Astoria with Sinatra's voice still ringing in my ears. It gave me a good feeling, and I was sort of daydreaming that I had been the one to stand up to Eddie, not realizing that I would have an opportunity hours later. After a few hours of sleep, I got a call from Eddie telling me that I had to come and meet him at the place by twelve noon and that it was important. I knew this had to do with the last night's episode, and on my way there, I started getting bad feelings about this meeting.

When I got there I found Eddie and his partner, the lawyer Alex Lenes, waiting for me, and Lenes immediately started questioning me. He said he wanted to get a good idea of what had happened with Eddie and Mr. Sinatra and wanted to hear my version of the events. There was a sense of purpose in his voice and questions, and I quickly understood that they were planning some sort of lawsuit against Sinatra. Instantly, I realized that I was the person who saw and heard everything, and I had all the information that they wanted. Immediately, I decided to lie rather than tell them anything. I knew I would probably lose my job, but because of Eddie's behavior toward the staff, I had started to consider leaving anyway.

"When Mr. Sinatra came in," I told them, "he went straight to the office and was talking with Mr. Eddie. I was carrying a tray full of glasses, I brought it to the kitchen, and I spent some time placing the glasses into the machine. Then I came back to the dining room and saw Mr. Sinatra leaving."

"Did you hear any loud voices? Any threats? Did you see any commotion?" Alex asked.

"No. I didn't hear anything like that," I told him.

Eddie now felt emboldened with a lawyer next to him. He lost his temper and started screaming at the top of his lungs.

"You're a liar," he said. "You were standing right there the whole time and saw everything."

ELEVEN DAYS TO THE PROMISED LAND

I stayed with my story, and there was nothing that could make me change it. Alex now started pressing me, talking like a lawyer and repeating the same question over and over, trying to set up a trap for me and nearly succeeding.

"Even if you were in the kitchen, you could still clearly hear Sinatra from there," Alex pressed on.

"No, I didn't hear a thing," I told him.

Then he asked me to follow him to the kitchen and told Eddie to start screaming and calling out names like Sinatra did to see if we could hear him. In the kitchen, to Alex's satisfaction, we could clearly hear Eddie's loud voice repeating Sinatra's name-calling.

"I will subpoena you, I'll put you on the stand, and if you'll lie under oath, you will go to jail," Alex threatened.

"That's Eddie screaming now. All this proves is that Sinatra wasn't yelling," I said. "You should subpoena Jose, the porter also. He was here in the kitchen with me the whole time, and he would tell you the same thing."

I took a chance saying that, knowing that they wouldn't want to bring Jose into this. Jose was in the country illegally, and for years, Eddie had been taking advantage of him, working him very hard and paying him very little and off the books. But my strategy worked well because it made Alex think like a lawyer. He asked me to go and wait in the dining room, and then he went into the office to have a conversation with Eddie.

A few minutes later, Eddie, who always had to have the last word, stormed out the office screaming at me.

"Get out of here," he screamed at me. "You're fired, and I don't want to see you here again."

"What? I won't be seeing you in court?" I asked sarcastically.

And having had the last word, I walked out of the By-Line Room smiling.

CHAPTER 20

Audie Murphy—The Great American Hero

After being fired from Mabel Mercer's By-Line Room, I was eager to find another job just like the one I had. I was spoiled, I suppose, making eighty to one hundred dollars a night. In reality, there were only two or three such places in New York, like the legendary Copacabana, the Rainbow Room, or Toots Shor's, and it was very difficult to get into those places unless someone like Father Poulos made a phone call.

I had seen Father Poulos months earlier; I went to his office one Sunday afternoon to thank him for his help. When I entered, he was on the phone talking to someone, and he waved me in to sit down, and while I was sitting there, I experienced something that I'd never forget. It had nothing to do with my story, but it's worth telling anyway.

As I was sitting there waiting, I couldn't help hearing everything he was saying to the person on the other end.

"My community is building the new St. Catherine's Church on Thirty-Third Street in Astoria, and because we have a major parking problem, I need your help," he was saying.

And after a pause to listen, he continued, "I have a solution. There is an empty building for sale near the church, and if the city buys this building and makes a municipal parking lot there and collects parking fees, except of course on Sundays, holidays, and other church functions, this will be a win-win situation for both the city and my community."

After another pause to listen again, his face lit up with smiles, like he knew his solution was accepted.

"Thank you, Mr. Mayor," he continued. "I can assure you that my community will appreciate your help."

I was impressed when I heard the word "mayor" and understood that he had accomplished what he wanted by making just one phone call. He then turned to me with a big smile on his face, and proud as a peacock showing off his colorful tail, he said, "That was Mayor Lindsay. Now we have parking for our church."

Not long after, that building was torn down and the ground was converted into a municipal parking lot. Even today, years later, I think of that conversation every time I pass by there.

Now, knowing that all that could happen with just one phone call from Father Poulos, I thought that I should go see him again to see if he could get me into one of those high-end places. But I couldn't bring myself to do it since I had just been fired from the By-Line Room.

So I began to assess my options. Since I met Audie Murphy in Fort Knox, I had often fantasized of someday going to California to reconnect with him again. Most of the time, it was just a silly thought, nothing that I would ever actually pursue. But I had found Audie to be a fascinating man and thought that we had a real connection in the short time that we spent together. And now, without a job, I seriously considered the possibility of making the trip.

I was in my early twenties, I had saved some money, and since I had heard so much about California and all the Hollywood glitz, I thought I could find a job just as good as the one I had in New York.

Although Audie Murphy and I were born a world apart, in those two days at Fort Knox, I believed we had felt a strong kinship for each other, maybe because during our conversations, we realized that we had lived similar lives. We both were born in small villages, me in the mountain village of Valtesiniko in Greece and Audie in the tiny rural town of Kingston, Texas. We both came from large families and lost our fathers before the age of ten, and we had both been forced to grow up fast in turbulent times. We had tasted the atrocities of war before the age of eighteen, spilled blood, and carried dark memories and haunting ghosts from fraught pasts.

But that was then, and now, I didn't even know if Murphy would still remember me. After all, he was America's greatest war hero and had become a very popular movie star. And because he had a busy life, I had many good reasons to believe that after four years, our three days in Fort Knox didn't linger in his memories as they did in mine.

Hoping that I was wrong, I packed my little suitcase and took a plane to Los Angeles anyway. The only place that I had heard about was Hollywood; so I got in a bus marked "Hollywood." After a long ride, the bus made a stop in front of the Commodore Hotel on Hollywood Boulevard, which was very convenient for a traveler like me looking for a place to stay. It was a very upscale, Hollywood-type hotel, and after I checked in, I found out it also had very upscale rates for my budget, so I decided to stay there only one night.

The next morning, I checked out, and from a telephone booth in the lobby, I dialed the number Murphy had given me four years earlier with very little hopes that he would remember me.

"Good morning. Mr. Murphy's office." It was a young lady's voice. Her friendly tone gave me some encouragement that I might get to speak with Murphy, and I explained who I was and that this number was given to me by Mr. Murphy personally to call. As it turned out, that was the number to Audie's office at Universal Studios, and by pure luck, I had called at the right time, as he was sitting in his office in between filming. The young lady transferred the call, and then I heard another voice.

"The Army let you out? Welcome to Hollywood," the voice said.

I recognized his voice right away. He clearly remembered me, and after warm greetings, Audie Murphy gave me an address in Toluca Estates and asked me to get in a taxi and go to his house where we would meet later.

I was excited about receiving such a warm welcome, but I did not want to go to his house with my little suitcase, so before I went, I had to find a cheaper hotel, maybe near his house where I could drop off my suitcase. I got in a cab and told the driver to take me to Toluca Road in Toluca Lake, and having no idea where that area was, I also told him to first to take me to a cheap hotel in that area. That cabby got a little baffled, having to pick up a customer from an upscale hotel, bring him to an exclusive area, and somehow find him a cheap hotel in between.

But after I explained my situation, he turned out to be very sympathetic and helpful. His name was Sausa, and he suggested driving around Universal Studios, where many hopefuls lived nearby in rooming houses, suggesting that maybe I could find a room there.

Sausa knew his way around well and drove me to the right area past Universal Studios to a long building that looked like a motel with a "Vacancy" sign in the window. And while Sausa waited, I went in with my suitcase, and the lady in charge said that the rates were eight dollars per day. It was perfect for my budget, all thanks to Sausa.

I didn't even look around, I was happy I had found a place to stay that I could afford, and I paid the lady the eight dollars, left my suitcase in a room, and had Sausa drive me to Toluca Road. As we were driving through the area of Toluca Estates, I was admiring the beautiful houses that surrounded us with their well-manicured lawns and extravagant facades. But what caught all my attention was a huge American flag flying above the trees on a pole more than seventy feet tall that could be seen from everywhere. I thought that it must be some official building, like the town hall or a court house.

When we entered Toluca Road, it was a dead-end road with a big ranch house deep at the end, secured by a big steel gate with the address posted on a brick wall on the side. I knew then we had arrived at Murphy's house. The flag that I had seen from the distance wasn't on any official building; it was on the lawn of Audie Murphy's house. After Sausa left, I rang a bell, the gate swung open, and I started walking toward the house. Just then, Audie Murphy came out, first sending a quick glance up to the flag, and then walking toward me.

"So you made it to Hollywood," he said, offering warm and sincere greetings. He made me feel very welcome, which was surprising, given that he was a big Hollywood star and I had only known him for three days prior to this meeting. After four years, it was as if nothing had changed. He still had the same old baby face and soft voice, the same kind personality that he had shown me at Fort Knox. The only thing I noticed that was different was a blue iron revolver that he had tucked into his belt, and I thought quietly that it must be a movie prop, remembering that he had just come from the studio, perhaps filming a Western movie.

We walked into the house, and I met Audie's wife, Pamela, a lovely lady, and his two young sons, James and Terry, about three and five years old. It was around 9:00 p.m. We had a nice dinner that Pamela had prepared, and we talked about our meeting in Fort Knox, and during our conversations, I said that I was hoping to stay in California, and I needed to find a job soon. I told him about the job I had at the By-Line Room, hoping to find one just like it in Hollywood. I had also mentioned that I was staying near Universal Studios, and he asked me to meet him there the next day, and that he might have a job for me.

From the minute I walked into the house, I never felt like a stranger. Audie and his family had welcomed me despite the fact that Audie and I had not spoken in years, and at the same time, he treated me like someone he had known for years. And somehow, I felt the same way. It wasn't like being in the company of a stranger, or like being in the company of one of the most famous people in the world; it was more like being at the Zappeion Greek restaurant in Astoria.

The one thing I noticed, however, was that through the entire time of my visit, dinner and all, Audie still carried that gun in his belt. No one ever mentioned anything about it. It seemed to Audie and Pamela a perfectly normal thing, as if it were a piece of clothing or an accessory.

The next day, I walked over to Universal, and I gave my name to the guard at the gate, who told me to go over to the studio's restaurant where Mr. Murphy would meet me. The studio was fascinating. It felt as if it were an endless structure, with sets representing a slew of scenic locales, like the whole world had been condensed into a single place. It was even more interesting when I passed through to the commissary, a massive cafeteria where extras and actors got their meals dressed in all sorts of crazy costumes. It felt like walking through a carnival.

I walked a short distance to the restaurant, which was much more upscale than the commissary, and it was pretty crowded with the executive crowd and established actors. I waited by the entrance until Audie Murphy came, along with another actor named Charles Drake, and two beautiful young actresses, all dressed in Western outfits. I had seen this actor before in Murphy's movie *To Hell and Back*, the story of Murphy's military life. Murphy introduced me as his Army buddy, and he introduced the two beautiful young actresses as Joan Evans and Virginia Grey. I soon learned that their cowboy outfits were for a movie they were filming entitled *No Name on the Bullet*, one of Murphy's popular movies. They were a friendly bunch, talking about life in New York and Hollywood.

"This is not the By-Line Room, but this is as good as it gets," Murphy said. "I can get you a job here, if you want."

By this time, I was overwhelmed with all I had seen there, the famous actors and actresses and producers, and I didn't hesitate to say yes. Murphy spoke with the manager, and I was told shortly after that I would start working there the next day. I smiled; it seemed that I had found California's version of Father Poulos.

After lunch, it was time for them to go back to their location to continue their filming, and Audie asked me to tag along. There, I experienced something that I never expected, and I couldn't believe what I was seeing. When they took their places and cameras started to roll, I was amazed to see how these same four people with whom I was sitting with earlier could seemingly transform themselves to the characters they were portraying on screen. They could make the elaborate sets come to life, the costumes feel authentic, stories and characters feel like real people. I was swept away by their talent and charm, and I could feel that longing feeling that I had felt several times before. I thought that maybe I'd be able to learn that craft. I was hearing those sirens calling me again.

In the coming weeks, those sirens would only get louder. My reunion with Audie Murphy, and my work in the studio's restaurant, where I had fleeting exchanges with some of the big stars of the era, names like Dan Duryea, Gia Scala, James Stewart, Tony Curtis, and more, all fanned the flames of a bourgeoning dream to become an actor. In the meantime, I was living in the rooming house with some other dreamers, but I spent most of my time at Audie's house, where I got a first-person perspective of the price of stardom, and eventually got to know the real Audie Murphy.

For Audie, his family was his life. His wife, Pamela, a former airline hostess, and his two sons, James and Terry, were his world. As a child, his father was a drunkard who had left his family behind, and when his mother died, Audie was left to support his family alone. Now, his most important mission was to give his wife and two sons the best lives they could ever imagine.

The large American flag he had installed in his lawn was a personal point of pride, and I couldn't help noticing that every time Murphy was coming or going, he always gave the flag a quick glance, like a quiet salute to a higher power. As I learned later, he included in his will that if his house was sold, the flag should remain in place.

I would see that same flag flying there proudly, more than fifty years later when I visited California again and drove by the house. It stood as proud as ever, and as I drove by, I gave it a quiet salute in memory of my friend, the great American hero.

Outside of Audie Murphy's house in Toluca Lake, CA

Audie was a guy who would never forget and never hesitate to reciprocate those who once lent him a hand, like the legendary actor James Cagney who, as I learned later, brought Murphy and his war fame to Hollywood to develop him into a major star through his production company. And there was a Texas businessman named James Sherry, who was a major investor in a movie called *Bad Boys*, and who gave Audie his first starring role that got the attention of Universal Studios, yielding Murphy's first long-term contract. In appreciation, Audie named his first son "James" after the two James who helped launch his career.

But prior to the *Bad Boys* movie, James Cagney developed his own production company, which the big studio haunches saw as a threat. They forced Cagney into bankruptcy, and he retired in Massachusetts at Martha's Vineyard, leaving Murphy without any job or support other than a small amount he was receiving from his retirement from the Army. He then decided to use his fighting skills and become a boxer and started to train at Terry Hunt's gym in Los Angeles. Since he couldn't afford a place to stay, Terry Hunt allowed him to sleep on a cot in the gym until he landed the role in *Bad Boys*.

But he never forgot Terry Hunt's kindness and named his second son Terry.

I often lost myself in Audie's library. I was overtaken by the collection of his prestigious medals that he had earned during World War II. Murphy was the archetypal soldier. He had earned thirty-three medals, including three Purple Hearts and the Congressional Medal of Honor. He also survived brushes with death caused by three major wounds, malaria, and gangrene.

He was welcomed home with much fanfare and hero's parades and became a celebrity, a household name, easily transferring his good looks and charm into a successful acting career. But none of this ever got to his head. Besides the severe post-war stress syndrome he inherited from the war, he always remained a plain, ordinary Joe at heart. But for some reason, in all this time, I never saw Audie without the gun tucked to his belt. I never mentioned anything about it until one day Pamela set me at ease.

"Don't be concerned about the gun. Audie can handle it. It's like a comfort zone to him. He even sleeps with it under his pillow. It's the post-war syndrome. And Audie handles it well."

There were times, however, when I could see Audie expressing symptoms from that post-war stress syndrome. Often, I would see Audie sweat and become nervous, uneasy, for no reason at all. I would watch him fumble quickly to swallow pills that he always had on him. Then he would lock himself in a room and stay there for hours. Other times, I thought it might be a good idea to coax him into opening up about his heroisms, but always he cut me short.

"The real heroes are those with the wooden crosses," he'd tell me.

Once, I asked him if it was the luck of the Irish that he survived the war.

"Maybe it was," he said. "But I believe it was my quick shooting, an ability to shoot fast that I developed as a ten-year-old, shooting rabbits for food in Texas. At that time, if I didn't shoot fast, I would lose my meal. In war I'd lose my life."

As quick as Murphy was with the gun, he was also quick with words. There is a well-known story about the time that Pamela took their dog Skip to the dog groomer, but the groomer didn't listen to her requests for how the dog should be groomed, and she became upset with him. The groomer didn't know who Pamela was and made some nasty comments at her that made her go home in tears. That made Murphy angry, and when he went to confront the groomer, the groomer recognized him and noticed the gun on his belt. After Murphy gave the groomer a piece of his mind, he left. But the groomer apparently held a grudge, or perhaps was looking to make a case against a big-time celebrity. And so, he called the police and reported that Audie Murphy fired a shot at him.

Audie was called to the precinct, and after questioning, he was let go, only to face a group of reporters outside waiting for his comments, and one reporter asked him about it.

"Mr. Murphy, did you really take a shot at that man?"

Murphy, cool as always, answered with his own question: "And if I did, do you think I would have missed?"

Mingling with stars in Hollywood gave me a taste for the glamorous life, but I noticed the dreamers who lived in the rooming house with me were barely getting by, working brief shifts as extras in movies and then sitting around waiting for their next break. They were struggling to make the rent and pay for their meals. I quickly saw that my chances of being an actor were slim and that, even if I had a chance, it was a volatile career that could be very short-lived. It was not the life I was looking for when I boarded the big ship to come to America.

Through Audie, I also saw glimpses of the Hollywood life that both excited and terrified me. I happened to be at his house one day when his agent, whose name I gathered was Al, came by with dollar signs in his eyes and started talking like a used car salesman.

"Murph, I got you the biggest deal ever," he said. "Big money. It's a big international company, and they want you to be their spokesman. I cut a good deal for you, with big money, Murph. All you got to do is say yes."

Murphy asked who the company was, but the agent just kept repeating his pitch: "It's a huge company, and they want a spokesman like you to be the face of the brand, with billboards all over the world."

"Who is this company?" Murphy asked again, serious now.

"Salem Cigarettes," the agent murmured.

For me, scraping by and considering chasing a career in acting, I stood there with awe and started to fantasize about the Hollywood lifestyle, having agents barging into your mansion with offers of big money and fame, to put your face on billboards all over the country. That's what I want to be some day, I told myself.

But then, Audie took me by surprise when he became uneasy with his agent. "So they want to use my image and pay me big money to tell the youngsters to smoke their cigarettes?"

Satisfied, the agent nodded with his head "yes."

Murphy then became agitated, stood up, and unleashed. "So you cut me a good deal with big money, and all I have to do is push cigarettes on all the youngsters who are there looking up to me. You should already know the answer to that, Al. It's the same answer I gave you before about the beer deal."

"But, Murph, let me tell you about the money," the agent insisted.

"Is that all you care about? Money? Haven't you made enough money all these years as my agent?"

"You already turned down the beer offer and now with this. Soon you'll get a reputation for turning down offers, and no one will consider you anymore. You've got to go with the flow in this town," the agent said.

"I am going with my own flow and my ethics," Audie answered. "You can take those kinds of offers to somebody who doesn't care. You can find plenty of those in this town."

This exchange continued for a while with arguments from both sides, and when the agent finally left, Murphy continued to educate me about the life in Hollywood.

"You can't be your own man in this business," he told me.

It was then that I realized that the Hollywood life was complicated, and it wasn't all about the fame and the money. It was intimidating and sleazy, and quietly, I began considering returning to New

York. Besides, I had noticed that California was a different animal. It was a slower life, and I missed the hustle and bustle of the Big Apple.

One day, I decided to ask Audie, who I saw as a big brother, for advice. He didn't answer right away. Instead, he suggested that we take a ride. We drove to the Santa Anita Racetrack and went in just as a race was starting. We watched the horses, all bunched up and curving around the stretch, as they vaulted toward the finish line. The jockeys whipped them frantically, eyeing victory before a hungry crowd.

"This is the actor's life, a horse race. Only one makes it to the winner's circle," Murphy said as we watched the horses battle each other and get whipped to win money for their masters.

"I've done my racing in the battlefields, and that's what got me here while others got left behind. I'll never dishonor them by pushing beer and cigarettes to our future soldiers for the sake of money. I can walk on my own path. As for you, get out of this Hollywood life while you still can."

With that sincere advice, I know that I had found my American brother, and it was Audie's brotherly words that sent me back to New York for good.

The day we were saying goodbye, he insisted that I take a fifty-dollar bill he was giving me, knowing that I would need it. We parted, but our friendship continued and never faltered. We communicated and saw each other on the rare occasion that he came to New York. Our friendship would have lasted forever, but unfortunately, it was cut short by Murphy's premature death in a plane crash on May 28, 1971 over the Virginia mountains at the age of forty-six.

I watched him be buried with full military honors at Arlington Cemetery in Washington D.C. America lost its hero, and I lost my American brother, but the country would never lose its hero. Still today, his gravesite is the second most visited behind President Kennedy.

Later, the only thing I could do for his memory was to join Congressman Vito Fossella from Staten Island, who had served with Murphy, in a nationwide movement supported by the *New York*

Daily News and veterans all across the country, to get the postal service to issue a stamp in Murphy's honor.

It was a hard four-year battle with the postal service.

"We don't want to remind people of wars." It was their constant argument as they kept issuing stamps with Disney characters and flowers.

But we had a stronger argument that ultimately convinced them: "It was not us who started the wars. It was us who finished them."

Finally, on May 3, 2000, Audie Murphy's stamp was unveiled.

TELEPHONE STanley 7-1211   CABLE ADDRESS UNFILMAN

UNIVERSAL PICTURES COMPANY, INC.
UNIVERSAL-INTERNATIONAL PICTU | ;
UNIVERSAL CITY, CALIFORNIA

January 2, 1958

Mr. Dean Pavlon
23-80 - 35th St.
Astoria, Long Island
New York

Dear Dean:

It was very kind of you to remember
us with that lovely Christmas card. Pam and
the boys join me in sending their thanks and
best wishes to you for the coming year.

Sincerely,

Audie Murphy

Letter from Audie Murphy

CHAPTER 21

New York, New York

When I came back to New York, I took a job in the Wall Street area, at a restaurant called Oscar's Delmonico. It wasn't quite what I had at Mabel Mercer's though. It was more like the restaurant I worked at in Universal Studios, a gauche lunch place catering to the Wall Street biggies. It was slow and classy, and things started to close down around 6:00 p.m. each night.

But the energy of supper clubs was in my blood. I was entranced with the late nights, the dimmed lights, and the drama that unfolded each evening. I missed leaving the club in the wee hours of the morning with the piano's notes still tingling in my ears like a record playing in my head on the subway home. Oscar's Delmonico had its moments, but it was like a secret gambling house, where the big stockbrokers and their rich clients came with serious faces to talk business and make their investment plans.

I often visited a place on Forty-Second Street between Broadway and Eighth Avenue called Hector's Cafeteria that stayed open all night. It was inexpensive and convenient, a good place to sit with a cup of coffee and unwind after work. It had become an informal headquarters for waiters working all hours in clubs and hotels around Manhattan. It was also a meeting place for young, aspiring actors and actresses, not the rich and famous, but the hoping-to-be rich and famous. It reminded me of my rooming house in California, filled with dreams, many of which would go on unfulfilled.

In my frequent stops there, I got to know just about everyone who came in, and I told them that I was looking to make the move from Wall Street to uptown, where all the night action was. And it paid off. One night, Tom Dillos, a regular at Hector's and a fairly close acquaintance of mine, rushed over to tell me that there was an opening coming up at the place where he was working called the Round Table on East Fiftieth Street.

Getting a job in an upscale supper club like that wasn't an easy feat; you had to be lucky or know the right people. Trying to get a job without a recommendation was like trying to get into a Broadway play without a ticket. So I didn't waste any time and made my way to the Round Table. It was a huge elegant place with booths all around and a dome-shaped ceiling with an impressively large chandelier hanging from the center. It was previously the site of the Versailles Theater, where famous singers, like the French singer Édith Piaf, once performed. After the theater closed down in 1958, the Roulette Record Company owners, including a man named Morris Levy, took it over and renamed it, planning to feature all the most well-known acts of the time.

I spoke to the maître d', a guy named Bruno Levy, and gave him my admission ticket. I told him that Tom Dillos had recommended me, and fortunately, that was enough for him, and I got the job. From the first night's work, I knew that I had finally landed where I wanted to be. The performer there was a well-known singer at the time named Mel Tormé, and the place was packed every night with high-class customers who made the work easy and were good tippers. Every night I fluttered from table to table like a hummingbird, happily serving people and picking up good tips.

On the second floor was a little room that was originally called the King Arthur Room, but different performers would perform there for a few months at a time, making it a sort of home that was modeled after their personalities. For a while, it was home to a Don Rickles-type comedian named Jackie Kannon. Kannon was a feisty comic whose jokes often came at the expense of his audience, especially those in the ringside. His domain was affectionately known as Jackie Kannon's Rat Fink Room, and every night, it was filled with customers who loved Jackie's off-color jokes. He was once kicked off the Ed Sullivan Variety Show for using words and gestures forbidden on television in those days.

I worked downstairs in the Round Table with Tom, Bruno, and others, so I rarely got to see Jackie's performances of harsh jokes. But one night, I saw a young O.J. Simpson, fresh out of the draft and playing for the Buffalo Bills, going upstairs to the Rat Fink Room, and after a short time, to everyone's surprise, he came running down the stairs and rushed out of the front door like he was running toward the end zone for a touchdown.

Later, Kannon came down in between shows, and I overheard him saying, "That O.J. is one bad ass kid."

And he didn't mean it as a compliment.

"He's just a rookie in a big city," Kannon added.

I suppose, he had cracked a joke about O.J.'s rookie year, and maybe O.J. didn't like being laughed at or wasn't good at taking a joke. Looking back on that moment, I've always thought that he may have not known how to fit in or how to take a harsh joke in a tough city filled with tough guys and scrappy survivors. Perhaps he was better suited for the slower life on the west coast, or perhaps it was foreshadowing something that nobody would know until years later: that O.J. wasn't particularly good at dealing with the issues in his own life.

But I realized something that day: New York is a great city for all who want to work and be happy. It can be tough and intimidating, but it's a fun-loving place that feeds off of embarrassment and self-abasement. There is no room for egos there. The comedians will pick on you, and the cab drivers will run you down.

CHAPTER 22

A Girl Named Agnes

Just as Hector's Cafeteria was our Manhattan meeting place, our meeting place in Astoria was the Neptune Diner. It was located in the hustle and bustle of Thirty-First Street, right next to the elevated subway stop on Astoria Boulevard. For the true Astorians, especially us Greeks, that diner was the center of our solar system. At that time, not everyone had a car, so the Neptune Diner was a convenient location, a nexus, for us to take the subway and meet there on our days off. There, we'd eat and then usually head back to somebody's house to play poker.

Most of the time, these informal casino nights, a tradition practiced by many Greek generations, would take place once a week in the basement at the house of a friend named Nick.

They were friendly games; we didn't play to win one another's money, but it was rather a chance to get together as a group, talk about girls, do some trash talk, have some laughs, and speak our own language. While poker was our most frequent activity, occasionally we changed things up, taking on a sport like bowling or soccer, and soon, these evenings became a tradition for us.

One night, as we entered Nick's house, I saw this beautiful young girl in her early twenties sitting in the kitchen with Mary, Nick's wife, having coffee. I had never seen her before, and Mary introduced her as Agnes, Nick's cousin visiting from Greece.

With her long black hair tossed over her shoulders, she was beautiful, carrying a look that seemed both friendly and smart. She sported a mysterious smile that made me wonder if she was a goddess who came alive and left the Parthenon to come to America.

At Universal Studios, I'd encountered some of the most beautiful movie stars of the era, the likes of Debbie Reynolds, Natalie Wood, Gia Scala, all of them elegant and classy, sometimes mysterious and complex. But this girl, here in Nick's kitchen, was now all that mattered to me. She had everything that those stars had without the ego that a life in Hollywood often breeds. She was friendly and sweet, and I knew I had to get to know her.

I never considered myself a shy guy, and when the others started to go down to the basement, I walked over to Agnes and Mary. Mary was always friendly with me, maybe because I'd always compliment her coffee when I walked into the house.

"Mary, your coffee, as always, smells delicious," I said as I often did.

I knew it felt forced, like bad writing in a TV show, but Mary was a smart lady, and I'm sure that she could figure out that my attention was trained on Agnes, and not on her coffee. She didn't play the part of the shepherd, shooing away the wolf to protect the innocent little lamb. Instead, she gave me an opening.

"Agnes made it," she said.

"That's very interesting," I said. "Agnes, you're here only a few days and already you know how to brew delicious American coffee? We need to talk about that."

Uninvited, I pulled up a chair and sat between them. I felt like I was soaring, like a missile, tearing through the clouds toward its target. Agnes gave me a smile, and the rest is history.

I never played cards again, and two months later, Agnes became my wife, and together we established the American Dream that we both wanted. I continued my job at the Round Table while Agnes worked for a watch company in Jackson Heights. Our dream would glow even brighter when we were blessed with our first baby girl, Effie, and again, four years later, when we welcomed our second baby girl, Olga.

With Agnes taking care of our little girls and me providing, we were building a life that neither of us had ever thought was possible.

I sometimes thought that we must have been destined to be together by fate. In many ways, we were the perfect picture of the American Dream: a small spoonful of that vaulted melting pot, two immigrants who had caved out their own little place in the greatest country on earth. It wasn't anything big and flashy, but it was the beginning of a new and wonderful life. We were unaware that soon, some friends from the past would step into our lives and take our dream farther than we could have ever imagined.

My wedding to Agnes

My daughter Effie

My daughter Olga

Olga's Wedding

CHAPTER 23

The Big Reunion

First, it was Mabel Mercer, who one day contacted me out of the blue, excited to inform me that Jackie Kannon was ending his long-time stay at the Rat Fink Room and that she'd be taking over, turning it into a smaller music lounge that would come to be known as Mabel Mercer's Room. I was pleasantly surprised when she offered me a position as the maître d' of her new spot.

That was the easiest decision that I would ever make. I was thrilled with the idea of reuniting and working with Mabel again. She treated everyone well, and now, the place would be under mine and Mabel's watch—no more Eddie trying to exert control over us—so I didn't hesitate to say yes.

By now, I had a pretty good idea of what it took to be a maître d' on the upper echelon of the club staff, the front end of the customer service experience. I'd be commanding a team of waiters, waitresses, and bartenders to make sure that each and every night in Mabel Mercer's ran smoothly. Back in the Army, when I was assigned to lead a team of rookies in building a baseball field, I was given a new pair of stripes. Now, once again, I'd be given a new uniform, and I rushed to buy my first tuxedo.

It took a few nights to convert the room to Mabel's style and atmosphere, and soon she was comfortable, sitting on her chair in front of the piano with her pianist, Sam, behind her. There was no microphone, no loudspeakers, only Mabel's singing and Sam's piano notes. When we were ready, we opened the doors, and just like that, Mabel Mercer and I were back, and this time on our own terms. On opening night, Mabel's loyal followers filled up the room just like in the old days.

It was around midnight when Mabel's most loyal follower, Frank Sinatra, came in with his all-star entourage: the legendary Sammy Davis Jr., the First Lady of Song Ella Fitzgerald, Tony Benett, and Jilly Rizzo, Sinatra's best friend and the owner of the famous club "Jilly's" on West Fifty-Eighth Street.

I knew that Sinatra had always reveled in Mabel's singing style. But even more, I had seen, firsthand, that Sinatra was an immensely loyal person. Friendship was like a sacred code to him, and he wasn't afraid to turn his quick temper toward anyone, like Eddie, that sought to hurt his friends.

I hadn't seen him since his altercation with Eddie a few years earlier, and I was thrilled to meet up with him again. I was standing by my desk near the entrance as they walked in, and he approached me like an old friend, catching me completely by surprise with a new nickname.

"Hey, Greek," he said, smiling, offering me a strong handshake followed by a warm hug. I had expected the handshake, but the hug and the nickname were all surprises, and for a few seconds, I was happily bewildered at how well he remembered me. Sinatra was known to give nicknames and friendly embraces to those who he liked. And now, I felt that I was among that group.

As I was greeting the others behind him, I felt that something had changed between us, and I wondered if he had somehow found out about how I had stood by his side in his confrontation with Eddie and the lawyer. I had only mentioned that to Mabel, and I suppose it was possible that she may have told him. But it was a question I'd never get the answer to though I always had my suspicions that he knew. For now, all I could do was perform my job as a maître d' as best I knew how.

"I'll show you to your table, Mr. Sinatra," I said.

He took one step closer to me and looked me straight in the eyes, conveying some vague sense of understanding. It had seriousness behind it, and I got a little startled, thinking that I may have said something wrong.

"To my friends, it's Frank," he said.

I felt a warm bond between us in that moment, but I was also conscious of who he was and my position in relation to him, so I just couldn't bring myself to call him Frank, not at that moment anyway. All I could come up with was: "Thank you. It's my honor."

I've always thought that there was something there in his words, his implication that I was a friend. He saw me as someone more than a working guy with a polite smile. I felt, and still feel, that there was a subtle agreement that I was on his side, and from now on, he would be on mine. And I knew Sinatra's loyalty meant something more than a handshake and a hug.

Since that time, for as long as I knew him, Frank was always immensely loyal, just as I'd seen in how he defended Mabel. And indeed, over the next few months, Frank came back frequently, and each time our friendship kept blossoming. We grew friendlier with each other, more open and trusting. He called me Greek, which meant a lot, because I could see that he gave nicknames to few. If Frank knew your name, that wasn't special because he knew everybody's name. You knew Frank thought you were special if he gave you a nickname, something that would separate you from the crowd, something that made you a friend. And over the years, his friendship forced me to redefine the word loyalty.

As I've mentioned, when Mabel sang, she never used a microphone, and the waiters stopped serving. As the maître d', I made sure of that. Mabel wasn't one for those metallic tones that diluted her notes. Her style and voice attracted attention, and beneath the spotlight, she crooned for a cool hushed crowd that sat hidden beneath dim lighting, hanging on each soothing utterance with a militant attention. There was no electronic middleman to muddy the spell, no waiters taking drink orders, no stray chatter at the tables—just magic. And nobody understood that more than Frank who displayed his loyalty once again when one night, he came in with a beautiful girl and I sat them in a booth together, side by side. When Mabel started singing, the girl was more interested in Frank than Mabel's performance. I could see her in the darkness, chattering to Frank, and each time, Frank would turn away slightly, gently shush her, and point to the stage. I could see him growing impatient.

When Mabel finished singing, she walked over to sit at Frank's table, and I followed behind to see if she wanted something. Frank was very serious as he introduced Mabel to his companion.

"This is Mabel Mercer. We call her mother because we all have one mother, and there's only one Mabel. We don't interrupt her singing," he said, firmly.

The girl must have seemed uninterested, or Frank must have not liked how she barely acknowledged Mabel, and for Frank, that was the last straw. He pulled a wad of hundreds out of his pocket, peeled off one, and handed it to me. "Greek, call a cab and give this to the driver. This girl is leaving."

The girl hesitated for a moment, but then she realized that she had crossed a line, and that it was Frank Sinatra issuing the orders. Quietly, she stood up to leave, and I escorted her down the stairs and out of the club to find Harry, or as I called him, "Punchy Harry," a limo driver and former boxer who I knew very well and could trust.

In his prime days as a fighter, Harry made a boatload of money for his handlers and managers. But now he was broke and making a living for himself by running a limo service using an old Cadillac. He was a humble, quiet, and trustworthy guy who appreciated any business sent his way, and with all the gossip columnists in New York City floating around like hawks, I felt that it was my job to insulate Sinatra from any sort of gossip or bad publicity, and I knew if any ugly rumors started to spread, Harry would be on our side.

I found him outside, sitting in his car and waiting for a fare; I gave him the hundred and told him to take the girl anywhere she wanted and to keep everything under wraps. I knew Harry understood.

My budding friendship with Sinatra also extended to his personal secretary, Dorothy Uhlemann, who I got to know very well. She was a special person who rose to be Sinatra's confidant and personal secretary for thirty-four years. Dorothy was a real New Yorker who grew up in The Rockaways, with a tough straightforward attitude. She traveled the world with her boss, dealing with presidents, kings, queens, prime ministers, and so many other notables. She was witty, smart, and tough enough to weather all storms, of which there were plenty. But her heart was always with the simple people.

One night, she came with her staff to hear Mabel sing, and she gave me an envelope with four front row tickets to Frank's upcoming concert at the Nassau Coliseum on Long Island. It also contained Frank's contacts for his Waldorf Astoria and California offices.

"Mr. S. wants you to have this," Dorothy told me.

That was a special moment for me. I took it as a seal to our friendship, and it made me feel important and honored. I kept the note with his information well guarded, knowing that someday, I could use it for something important.

CHAPTER 24

The Vision

Working with Mabel again, I felt that I had returned to a home that I never even realized I'd lost, and I knew I had landed somewhere even better than the Round Table, but it was ultimately cut shorter than I'd hoped. To my surprise, an aging Mabel Mercer announced that she would be retiring soon with plans to return to her native England and perform only on special occasions. It came as an unfortunate surprise to me because, not only was I losing a good friend in Mabel, but I'd also be losing a job that I'd loved. I made sure to tell Tommy and Bruno that I'd still be available to work with them after Mabel's retirement. Little did I know that an old friend would be coming with another offer.

Back at the By-Line, there was a guy who came by often who I got to know as Jimmy Weston. Jimmy was a dapper, upbeat, funny guy who was known for wearing tailored suits or sports jackets and always had a smile plastered on his face. He hung around the bar, and if you ever heard laughter, he was always at the center of it: a knock-around New Yorker that you couldn't help but root for. He reminded me of Elias on the *Italia*, and eventually we became friends.

I got to know him as an undercover cop, but I couldn't imagine him arresting anybody. Maybe there was an edgier cop in there too that I had never seen. Supposedly, he did a lot of undercover work and spent a lot of his time jumping from club to club around the city, getting the lowdown from the locals and feeding his quiet passion for upscale jazz lounges and New York City's nightlife.

I would see Jimmy a few times at the Round Table as well, and when we opened the new Mabel Mercer's Room, he started coming in more often. And one night, when Sinatra was there, he asked me to introduce him.

The introduction was particularly warm, especially when I told Frank that Jimmy was a good friend and a cop, knowing that Frank was very fond of cops. I could tell that Jimmy appreciated that and was impressed to see that my relationship with Sinatra was more than just a relationship between a maître d' and customer.

One night, after Mabel retired and I was working downstairs again, Jimmy came in. But this time, he was all business and started telling me that he had retired from the police force and had opened a restaurant on West Fifty-Six Street, but the place was too small for his plans. He had found a bigger place, and he wanted to show me.

I thought he was looking for a friend's opinion, and I agreed to meet the following afternoon at 131 East 54th Street, just a few blocks over from the Round Table. It was the site of an old steakhouse called the Chateaubriand that had just closed down. When I got there the next day, he was already standing outside, flashing that big smile at me, and he took me inside where he began painting a picture of a future I had never expected.

"I think this place could be perfect for what the city needs, and believe me, I know the city," he said.

For years, there were many clubs in New York City where the biggest and brightest folks enjoyed listening to famous singers, danced to live jazz, and gossiped with cocktail glasses in hand. The big places, like Copacabana, or Toots Shor's, would attract all the biggest sensations. Sinatra and Joe DiMaggio spent a lot of time at Toots Shor's, and Copacabana welcomed everybody who was anybody. I spent some time at Toots Shor's and knew the owner, Bernard "Toots" Shor, pretty well. He called anyone in his restaurant who wasn't a celebrity a "civilian."

But by this time, the big-time entertainers had become very expensive, and clubs like the Copa had ether shut down or shifted to a newer audience of younger stars and thrill seekers, who were all becoming enchanted with the emerging dance music trend of disco. Toots Shor's, meanwhile, had closed after some trouble with the IRS.

The days of the snappy cool supper clubs were quickly giving way to a new generation with more flash and empty flair, and for stars like the Sinatras, the Anthony Quinns, the Joe Dimaggios, and the Jackie Gleasons and all of New York's elite, there was no place left for them to spend their evenings, at least not like they once knew. And no one had their finger on the pulse of all these trends like Jimmy did.

"This could be the next Copa and Toots Shor combined. This is what New York City is missing," Jimmy said with confidence.

He was talking a mile a minute, pointing out the size of the place and getting excited about his vision for it, and I could see his point. The place was spacious, with a dividing wall that separated the dining room from the bar and the cocktail lounge, which were off to the left as you walked in. The wall itself was not totally solid; it was made up of long vertical oak strips, like wooden blinds, which left slits so those at the cocktail lounge could peer into the dining room but not get the whole picture. It kind of teased you, enticed you to enter.

"Together, we can do this," Jimmy kept saying, sure of himself. "I know a lot of people in the city that I can pitch this idea to. A place where they can find what they are missing: stiff drinks, good food, along with live music and dancing, like nowhere else in the city. And with you and your experience as our maître d', there'll be nothing but grand slams here."

I could see Jimmy's vision, clear in front of me, and as he was talking, I lost myself in a dream, seeing myself thriving in such a place. I knew then: that's where I wanted to be.

Coming to America, I remember talking to my co-travelers on the *Italia*. We all had the same dream: work hard and be successful. But none of us knew how. Most of us would go on to work in diners or coffee shops, where the sponsors who came before us had worked or were lucky enough to own.

Others went into construction or painted houses or got jobs in factories. No one came here with any clear idea of what their job, or their dream, would be. But for me in that moment, standing in that place with Jimmy, I saw my path for the first time. This was it. From early on, the excitement of the supper club world had drawn me in like a moth to a flame. It was an addicting lifestyle in some ways, bringing you within reach of power and fame and money and all the glamour and glitz that came with it. It allowed me to fantasize about a different life; it let me feel like a movie star, even if my name had never appeared in the credits. Even more so, it made those names feel more human and down to earth in a way that few would ever witness.

Jimmy knew I had a very good relationship with Sinatra, and he knew that it could be crucial for a new place to have Sinatra come in as a friend and customer. And once the word was out, the place would be jammed every night.

But as an undercover cop, he was also good at getting reads on people. He had seen something in me that I had only vaguely seen in myself: that I loved the nightclub business, that this was not just a job to me. It was my passion, my craft, and that passion could be the difference between failure and success.

My vision was colliding with Jimmy's vision, and in my excitement, I could hear my own voice telling me that this wasn't a dream. This was the real deal, and I couldn't wait to plan the next step.

However, in all the excitement, I hadn't given a thought to my biggest obstacle: money, and suddenly, that hit me like a summer thunderstorm. I had been making good money supporting my family, and anything extra I made was sent back home to Greece, where my family relied on me for support.

Jimmy kept talking, but now I was less excited, and I just stayed silent like a defeated warrior. As he went on, I felt that I should tell him. After all, he had chosen me, and I just couldn't let him keep on building his dream, only to let him down.

Finally, I took a deep breath and got some courage to speak. "Jimmy, I love this idea, but I don't have that kind of money," I told him, hoping to hear that he had all the money that was needed.

Jimmy looked at me, giving that smile he always had.

"You know something? Neither do I!" he said, and we both burst into laughter.

Neither of us could find the right words after that, but instead, silently, we realized we were sharing the same dream. We had no money, but we had a dream, and on that day in 1969, Jimmy Weston's Supper Club was born. I didn't know it then, but Jimmy was right. Inside those walls, some of the most exciting chapters in America's entertainment history would be written.

For twenty years, that club would be the prime watering home for all the famous and infamous: the fiery leaders like Yankees owner George Steinbrenner; the unlikely poets like the great Muhammad Ali; the cops and robbers like Bo Dietl, Sonny Grosso, and John Gotti; the everyday New Yorkers; and of course, my friend Frank Sinatra.

A gift from Mr. Sinatra to my daughters, Effie & Olga

F_S

February 8, 1994

Dear Dino,

Thank you very much for your special birthday
gift! I appreciate all the time and effort
that went into making it especially for me
and I thank you for remembering me in such a
thoughtful way! It's a marvelous tribute and
I thank you for your very kind words -- and
generous support!

I send my warmest good wishes to you and your
daughters, Effie and Olga!

All the best,

Frank Sinatra
Frank Sinatra

Letter from Frank Sinatra

CHAPTER 25

The Perfect Team

As it turned out, Jimmy was right to be confident in his knowledge of New York City. He had contacts in every circle, every tier of life in the city, from his buddies in the NYPD to the club owners to politicians, Wall Street honchos, big businesses, and average Joes. He had a pulse on everything that was going on, and he knew the ingredients to producing the next hot spot. And with that trademark grin and overflowing positivity, he could market those ingredients effectively to interested investors. I wasn't too involved in that part of our enterprise, but he drew from his reputation as a hardworking, honest guy, using his boundless optimism to make them believe in our dream.

It was so hard to argue with him, to doubt him, or pop the bubble of optimism that he seemed to carry around like a little kid with a balloon. Jimmy enticed them by painting the same picture he had painted for me of a new club that would be the center of life in New York City. Everyone wanted to root for us, and we didn't have to work too hard, and soon we were like a hot commodity on Wall Street. We'd build our dream on the backs of silent investors who had put their trust and money on us.

We put our ideas together, we hired the right people, and we transformed the place from a regular restaurant to a supper club. We eliminated some tables to make room for a round dance floor and a bandstand with a big Steinway piano and a sound system. We added some plush decor, a new carpet, and candlelight lamps on each table encased by translucent red domes, and we reupholstered all the booths.

But one thing was overlooked. The place previously didn't have any music, and when we tested the sound system, the sound bounced off the wooden walls in disarray and sounded awful. We hired a sound technician who found a quick fix; he installed heavy pleated fireproof curtains to dull the sonic impact, adding a deep red to the color scheme. The exterior was decorated with a large green awning extending over to the street with light letters that read: *Jimmy Weston's*.

Jimmy brought in the kitchen staff from the small restaurant he owned on Fifty-Sixth Street along with Nick Pappas, a great guy in his sixties who would take on the maître d' duties with me. My job was to assemble all the rest of the help we needed, and I contacted waiters and bartenders I had worked with in the past to put together a group that I was comfortable with. The first guy I chose was Tom Dillos, who got me the job at the Round Table. There were others like Suazo, Pete Prosalentis, Joe La Franka, and Antonio Diaz. For captains: a guy I knew at the Round Table named George Pappas (no relation to Nick Pappas), and Joe Rivera, who I met at Toots Shor.

Choosing bartenders required more selectivity because we knew it would take a special character to tend the bar in a special place like ours. To be a good bartender, make good tips, and bring money in for the house, you have to like what you're doing and have the personality to go with it. Remembering names, being cheerful, and having a good sense of humor was important. Even more important was being okay with being trapped behind the bar, listening and talking to your customers whose characters could change after a few drinks.

Jimmy, as a bar hopper most of his life, got know the right ones, guys like Joe Mayo, Big Mike McAren, Patty Quinn, Jo Babock, and Bobby Melvin. We brought them all in.

There was a piano singer named Tommy Furtado who Jimmy liked. He was playing at a club called the Gaslight, and Jimmy and I went to see him. He had a strong but mellow voice that you could never get tired listening to. During his break, we told Tommy that we were about to open a new supper club, and he agreed to put together a trio and come aboard. From opening night until closing night twenty years later, Tommy and his band would be our house band, sharing the stage with other musicians and filling the place with good music from 8:30 p.m. till 3:30 a.m.

Meanwhile, everything else we added was decorative, and those would change throughout the years. Later, when the place was up and running, we struck up a relationship with artist Fay Moore, whose horse racing and sports paintings would grace our walls for years. Hidden in the corners of those works were small price tags, and customers were welcome to purchase the art.

When I was sure that everything was up and running well and our clientele was starting to build up, I pulled out the envelope that Dorothy Uhlemann had given me and wrote Sinatra a note.

"I am at a new place called Jimmy Weston's on 131 east 54th Street. Please stop by when you are in town. It'll be good to see you again," I wrote.

Knowing Sinatra's loyalty, I was certain that he would come, but I didn't say anything to Jimmy because I wanted to surprise him.

One night, when the place was filled with a decent-sized crowd of average Joes, Sinatra showed up, trailed by Dean Martin, Sammy Davis Jr., and his old pal Jilly Rizzo.

When they walked in, it was like the air had been suddenly sucked out of the place. All of the chatter and the laughter at the bar went silent, and everybody's attention turned to Sinatra and his all-star entourage. Some stared with eyes wide open, starstruck. The dancers on the floor all stood still, breathless and looking with awe, as others walked by slowly, stealing glances.

"Hey, Greek, how are you?" Sinatra said with his usual hug.

Jimmy rushed over from the bar, just as wide-eyed as all of our customers, anxious to meet his celebrity customers, and I reintroduced him. Then I escorted Sinatra's party to Table 17, a round table near my desk that was somewhat apart from the rest, offering them a degree of privacy. They sat there, talking, laughing, and smoking deep into the night, bringing a new kind of atmosphere of class and elegance to the place. And as long as they stayed, no one else would leave until the wee hours of the morning.

After that night, Table 17 became Frank's table. And with his stamp of approval, a table at Jimmy Weston's became the hottest ticket in town, and I was there, calling all the shots. As the word spread around, every night, someone new came in and turned heads. But it was that first night in 1969 that started it all. Frank Sinatra, Dean Martin, Sammy Davis Jr., and Jilly Rizzo. What more could you ask you for?

Things happened fast after that. Every night, the place attracted fun-loving people who came to flock around whichever celebrities were there, and while Jimmy Weston's would establish a solid crew of regulars, every night, there was someone different, top movie stars, singers, athletes, politicians, and the top mafia bosses who liked to show off their pinky rings and expensive suits. For many, it became a home away from home, where stories were told and often created, and where one could always retreat for a laugh and a beer with a rag-tag family of stars and fans.

But the legend of Jimmy Weston's didn't simply just happen. It took a vision and a dream. But most of all, it was the chemistry between Jimmy and me. We were a perfect team of two dreamers with the ambition of twenty.

CHAPTER 26

Table 10: The Birthplace of Monday Night Football

Shortly after we opened, Jimmy Weston's became the birthplace of a beloved sports tradition: Monday Night Football. It was one of our club's earliest claims to fame, and it kicked off two swinging decades' worth of other interesting, funny, and legendary moments.

It all started in late 1969 with one of our most loyal customers—a real pleasant guy and a sports genius named Roone Arledge. He was the president of ABC's sports division, and he would often set up shop at our place, huddling alongside like-minded business pioneers over at Table 10, a corner, round table off to the left side of the room that was a popular spot for those who wanted privacy.

Every night, I would escort Arledge and another one of our regular customers, Howard Cosell, to Table 10, where they'd huddle for hours. Cosell was a famous sportscaster with a reputation for being confrontational and tough. He was famously known for being a no-nonsense, "tell it like it is" sort of journalist, and he always did just that. He was a truth seeker who could ask the hard questions to even the biggest sports stars, and he wasn't afraid to call out the fakers.

I remember him better for his endearing relationship with Cassius Clay, a young fighter out of Louisville, Kentucky, who would later change his name to Muhammad Ali and take the boxing world by storm. Ali was a young and athletic boxer with the build of a Titan and the wit of a poet. Cosell was an older fast-talking man who often came across as strict or cranky.

When these two were together, they were hilarious and never ceased to entertain the crowd, like each time they held interviews, during which Ali would reach over and pretend to remove Cosell's hairpiece. Cosell would feign anger and get into his best boxing pose as the two would exchange playful jabs. Their interviews were similarly peppered with verbal jabs, and each interaction ended in laughter. However, you could see the admiration and respect they held for each other.

Those meetings between Roone Arledge and Howard Cosell went on for a couple of weeks, and then, two of my favorite football players would join in on the huddle. One was a well-known former wide receiver for the New York Giants, Frank Gifford, and the other was then-famous Dallas Cowboys quarterback Don Meredith, who Cosell affectionately nicknamed "Dandy Don."

Their dinner and drinks always seemed like a friendly, social gathering, just four people enjoying a night out in New York City. But occasionally, I could tell, the conversation would pass into brief moments of seriousness, and it was in those moments that I knew something big was cooking over at Table 10.

Times, then, were different than they are now; it was possible for the common person to catch glimpses of world-shifting deals, as they played out, nearly undetected, in the public eye. Business wasn't reserved for plush offices, hidden behind closed doors, where executives and investors played white-collar war games and made cutthroat power plays. Instead, business was commonly conducted over dinner tables or at cocktail lounges in executives' favorite watering holes. Those were times when promises and handshakes over drinks were as good as signed contracts. Integrity, trust, and honesty were as valuable as money.

That's the way it was, and I remember it well.

When I first came to America, I remember sitting next to my uncle George, who was watching a football game. I had no idea what was going on in the game, but I was captivated by the players' sheer strength, their ability to think quickly under pressure, and most of all, their professionalism. After each aggressive play, the players handled themselves with class, even after viciously tackling one another down to the ground. There were no curses and no fights, no disrespect between competitors. Instead, they would congratulate one another.

I had come from an uncivilized, violent world, where one could get killed because of their beliefs, and as I was adjusting to life in a new country, I took comfort in the civilized manner of the players. I quickly became a fan of the game of football, and when Frank Gifford and Don Meredith would come to meet with Roone and Howard, it was always exciting for me, and I was always eager to talk with them about football.

Roone must have noticed my affinity toward the sport, because one night, as the "knights" of Table 10 were leaving, he stopped in front of me with his ever-present smile, perhaps a little brighter than usual.

"How would you like to see a football game every Monday night?" he asked.

What?

I was stunned. At the time, a football game on Monday night was unheard of. "Really? A football game on Monday night?" I asked in disbelief, hoping to hear more.

"We just closed the deal, and it will happen as soon as the season starts," he said with an air of confidence.

I congratulated him and told him I was excited about the idea. But initially, I was unsure of whether it would be successful, and when the official announcement came out, I remember hearing many negative comments. People thought that after a full weekend of games between both college and the NFL, the market of viewers interested in yet another game at the start of the workweek would be thin. Many thought that it wouldn't last.

But when it came to the business of football, Roone Arledge had a magic touch, and as it turned out, he once again knew exactly what the football world needed. He always pressed all the right buttons at all the right times, and this time was no different.

On September 21, 1970, as commentators Howard Cosell and Don Meredith first took their famous spots behind the microphones in Cleveland, Ohio, where the Cleveland Browns were set to take on the New York Jets, millions of fans took their places on their couches, in front of their TV sets to watch history in the making. And soon, all the football widows who lost their husbands every weekend to the NFL found themselves sitting on the couch as well, enjoying the fun.

Every Monday night at Jimmy Weston's was like New Year's Eve in Times Square. The cocktail lounge was always packed wall to wall with drinking fans, their eyes glued to the TV, like they were seeing the New Year's ball coming down. Joe Marino, a bookie, set up shop there and took bets on each and every play of the game, from the coin toss to the final score.

Monday nights changed forever both in the sports world and at Jimmy Weston's. The happy hour never ended, it went on throughout the game and long after, with the winners celebrating and buying drinks for everyone else, and the losers meanwhile would stick around sulking and drinking, analyzing each decision made like true Monday morning quarterbacks.

And for me, today's Monday Night Football games have a special meaning. They bring me back to Table 10, where I witnessed the birth of Monday Night Football.

CHAPTER 27

The Swinging Years

The beginning of 1970 was, what I call, the start of the swinging years. It all started with Frank Sinatra, Dean Martin, Sammy Davis Jr., and Jilly Rizzo inaugurating the place, continued with the Monday Night Football, and then snowballed into a series of legendary moments and incredible celebrity encounters. For the next nineteen years, it became a place where countless celebrities of varying magnitude sought to enter an exclusive New York City oasis noted for its friendly atmosphere, snappy jokes, good drinks, bear hugs, and jazz. They were the best years of my life.

When I think back on it now, I can't think of a single dull night or any big celebrity or athlete, or any famous personality at of the time that didn't come through the place. Muhammad Ali, George Steinbrenner, Brooke Shields, Richard Nixon, Joe Frazier, Gregory Peck, Liza Minnelli, Sammy Davis Jr., Jackie Kennedy, Kirk Douglas, Betty White, Billy Martin, and so many more. Some became acquaintances with me, and others became the most valued friends that I would ever know.

That included Frank Sinatra, who in many ways was the center of our world and one of my closest friends. After his first visit, Frank quickly made Jimmy Weston's his favorite spot, and he always dropped in every time he came to New York. I also kept a close relationship with personal secretary Dorothy Uhlemann, who kept me in the loop on when he was coming to town so I could keep his favorite Table 17 open for him and his guests, like Sammy Davis Jr., Spiro Agnew, or Jackie Kennedy.

Table 17 soon gained a reputation, and when Frank wasn't in town, only the best and brightest stars could sit there. One of those was the always-entertaining Muhammad Ali. Ali was like a poet, he was as quick with his words as he was with his fists, and if you gave him an opening, he would fly away like a butterfly, dropping an onslaught of jokes with a wit as sharp as a bee sting, fascinating the crowd.

In those years, Ali had some big fights with the very tough and popular heavy weight champion of the world, Joe Frazier. They had three brutal fights with each other, landing them in the hospital each time afterward. But if you knew them, you couldn't help but notice the admiration and respect they had for each other outside the ring, often poking fun at each other with playful banter and joking trash talk.

One night, before one of their famed fights, Ali was at Table 17 with the fight promoter Don King and Howard Cosell, and I asked him if he was ready to fight Joe Frazier. Always ready, Ali jumped at the opportunity like he had been waiting for such an opening. He stood up and yelled at the top of his voice, catching everyone's attentions.

"I am ready for Joe Frazier right now," he screamed.

He knew that Joe often came to the place also, and he started scanning the crowd jokingly, as if searching for him.

"Has anybody seen Joe Frazier? If you see him, tell him I'm looking for him."

He continued to amuse the crowd, all the while promoting their big fight, while Don King sat there, loving every moment of it, as Ali continued on. "Joe Frazier is so ugly, and I won't let him mess up my pretty face. Joe is too slow, and I'm so fast, I can play ping-pong all by myself...I'm so fast, I can turn off the light switch in my room, and I'm in bed before the light goes out..."

In the meantime, the crowd went into hysterics that seemed to linger long after Ali left for the night and into the wee hours of the morning. No complaints from Jimmy and me. Moments like these were the best publicity we could ever hope for. They made the place incredibly popular, and the swinging years began to roll.

Another pair that brought thrills to Jimmy Weston's was Neil Armstrong and Buzz Aldrin, the first two humans to land and walk on the moon. It was their first public appearance after their historic 1969 moonwalk after a thirty-day quarantine. They came in unannounced one night and received a remarkable standing ovation with thunderous applause, setting the place abuzz with excitement. Our customers relished the notion that they were in the presence of two men who had just returned from the moon.

There were no cell phones in those years, and at one point, Buzz Aldrin needed to make a telephone call, and he asked me if he could use my desk telephone, but the place was so noisy with excitement, making it very difficult for him to hear. So I offered to escort him up to our office for privacy.

I remember Buzz Aldrin as a very sociable, talkative person who appreciated my offering. We had a nice, interesting conversation, and at the end, he scribbled down my name and address. A week later, I was surprised to receive a package from Mr. Aldrin containing a picture taken on the moon and a golden keychain with an emblem, featuring the Apollo 11 and the American eagle. I'll always treasure that.

The news of their visit spread quickly throughout town, and one night sometime later, it came up in a conversation with Jimmy Weston, Jilly Rizzo, and Frank Sinatra. Sinatra was a deep admirer of the two pioneering astronauts and the story of their historic moon landing. I could hear him gushing with pride over the achievement, and the way he described it has always stuck with me. "It's such a historic achievement that it's hard to comprehend how it happened," I heard him say. "It's like the 1821 Greeks who, after four hundred years under the Turkish occupation, managed to preserve their culture and rise to freedom. A mind-boggling achievement."

I thought it was a fitting tribute to our hero astronauts, who had accomplished something of massive, historic proportions. And as a Greek, I was proud to hear that the legacy of Greek civilization would be held on the same level.

Some celebrities brought so much buzz in with them, but other than Neil Armstrong and Buzz Aldrin, only two others received thunderous applause when they'd enter or leave. It always happened with Frank Sinatra and Yankee owner, George Steinbrenner.

But one night, a different guest got a big applause.

It was some time after Watergate, and ex-President Richard Nixon and his entourage had stopped by the place, enjoying themselves until around midnight when they got up to leave. I stood by my desk waiting for them to pass so I could say good night. However, as they were walking through the dining room, the crowd started to applaud. And when they reached my desk, Nixon stopped in front of me and shocked me with a question of genuine surprise. "Why the applause? Is it because I am leaving?" he asked, smiling.

"Our customers always applaud for notables, Mr. President," I told him.

To this day, I still can't forget that strange look he gave me when he heard the words "Mr. President." It was like he was looking, searching to find out if I truly meant it. At that moment, I actually felt sorry for him. It was sad seeing the once most powerful man in the world, who had fallen so hard, looking for some compassion. I think he must have felt comfortable with me at that moment.

"I'd like to send something to you. May I have your name?"

"Of course, Mr. President," I told him, and he wrote down my name and my home address, and about a week later, a heavy package arrived containing a large book. It was an autographed copy of his memoir; it's a large book with such small letters that it's difficult to read, but I read most of it.

I truly believe Nixon was like an altar boy compared with some of today's politicians, who, as we now know, have committed more serious crimes that were never punished.

It wasn't just celebrities and big names that created the swinging years; it was also the selection of entertainment that enticed New Yorkers to come every night and drink and dance until the morning hours, when the lines between yesterday and tomorrow blurred. Our house singer Tommy Furtado gained many fans, but his biggest was Sinatra, who admired his voice so much, he dubbed him with the nickname "Pipes." Tommy shared the stage with other fine singers, like one named Mike Ceratti, and Billy Daniels, who would bring down the house with his big hit "That Old Black Magic."

Other big names would take the stage occasionally, too, like Arvell Shaw, a bassist known for playing in Louis Armstrong's band. And to add variety to the entertainment, we created special Wednesday Jazz Nights with Woody Allen, who, aside from acting and directing films, also led a jazz group he called the "New Orleans Jazz Band."

There was no other place in New York City that offered such variety of entertainment and attracted such a wide array of music lovers, and the swinging years continued on, bringing in plain people and notables alike. Johnny Carson, for instance, was there for many nights before he moved his ever-popular TV show to California. I remember Johnny as not much of a drinker, unlike his sidekick Ed McMahon, who could put his martinis away faster than the bartender could shake them. Johnny instead spent much of the time on the bandstand, to the delight of the crowd, doing what he loved best: playing the drums.

On a few occasions, there were some down, but funny moments, when the governor of New York State, Hugh Carey, after a few drinks, thought he could sing and would join Tommy on the bandstand. And that's when the dancers would take a break, still having fun, snickering from their tables at the governor's expense.

The mega movie star of that time and ever-popular artist Anthony Quinn also made the place his favorite stop, and he was always ready to be the life of the party. Anthony and I became close friends, and I still keep in touch with his family to this day. I called him "Patrioti," which in Greek means "compatriot." It signaled a special bond among Greeks, but actually, Quinn's heritage was Irish and Mexican. However, many people believed, and still believe, he was Greek because of his convincing performance in his signature movie *Zorba the Greek*, which earned him an Emmy nomination in 1964.

Anthony was always full of energy and liked to live his life to its fullest. When he was in the place, he'd come to me and say, "Dino, let's dance the Zorba dance."

And we'd rush into the dance floor, arms linked in the air. It happened so often that the regulars would come to expect it whenever Quinn walked in, and they'd all join in and dance with us. Those dances brought the best out of everyone in the place; it was like one big joyful New Year's Eve party.

When I think of Jimmy Weston's, I often revisit a column that I have in my collection by Paul Schwartzman from 1997 in the *New York Daily News*. It was an obituary, written after Jimmy's death:

> Night after night, Jimmy Weston's was a place for snappy conversation and epic storytelling, a place where someone was always buying a round at the bar and where lighters would flick to the ready if someone pulled out a cigarette.

It's a description that calls everything to life. Even now, I can see Jimmy, weaving and nudging between shoulders, living his dream and looking dapper as ever, that smile cemented on his face. When you walked into the place, it felt like you entered into Jimmy's big crazy family. The air was thick with laughter, and in every corner, there was likely someone that you knew, or an old friend from a past long forgotten. And even among strangers, the place fostered a special kind of kinship, some exciting, friendly energy that seemed to absorb all who entered.

I wouldn't be surprised if we were the inspiration to the theme song from the TV series *Cheers:*

> Sometimes you want to go where everybody knows your name, and they're always glad you came.

So many people came through there. Who knows? Maybe the guy who wrote that theme song was one of them. It was a place where nobody had a chance to order their own drinks because as soon as they sat down, a waiter would arrive with a tray of drinks, compliments from friends at another table.

A cocktail mix of stars, sports figures, dealmakers, politicians, and fun-loving socialites, a colorful cross section of a diverse city, a melting pot filled with the rich and famous, and the everyday Joe who just wanted a drink. Astute tourists, if they knew who to ask, would put a star next to Jimmy Weston's on their maps, and we often welcomed people from abroad who'd quickly learn that we weren't very different from one another, and we all wanted one thing: a good time.

I consider myself very fortunate to have been a part of that carefree wonderful world and to have taken part in the priceless, compelling, hilarious, stories still to be told in the chapters ahead.

I'm awed, sometimes, that a Greek immigrant who had fled war, tragedy, and poverty, had somehow ended up with a beautiful family at home and a strange extended family at work. Many times, at closing, I would wish that the night had never ended.

With Kathy Quinn

With Anthony Quinn

With The Boss George Steinbrenner at Yankee Stadium

The Champ Muhammad Ali

Second Man on the Moon Buzz Aldrin

With Yankee Great Phil Rizzuto

With Boxing Champion Joe Frazier

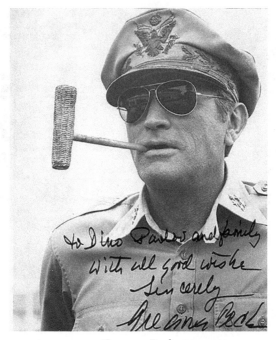

Gregory Peck

With ex-NYC Detective and Film Producer Sonny Grosso who
inspired the Oscar winning film The French Connection

Forever Popular TV Host Johnny Carson

With Greek Actress Katerina Lehou in Athens, Greece

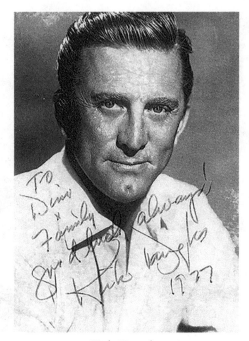

Kirk Douglas

With Nancy Sinatra at dedication of The Frank Sinatra
High School of the Arts in Queens, NY

With Tony Bennett at dedication of The Frank Sinatra
High School of the Arts in Queens, NY

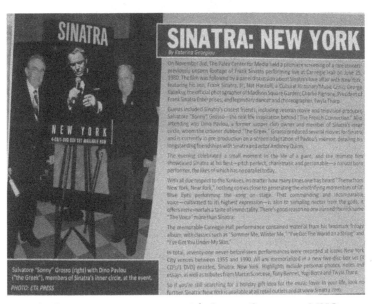

At Sinatra screening event with Sonny Grosso, ex-NYC
Detective and Film Producer Sonny Grosso

Headline from a magazine spread

CHAPTER 28

The Talk of the Town

In my twenty years as the gatekeeper of the most popular watering hole of the era, there's one story that I'll always love to tell. It was so funny that it quickly spread like wildfire all over the city, and it became the talk of the town. Years later, it surfaced again in a newspaper column.

It involved Frank Sinatra; the legendary baseball manager Leo Durocher; our men's room attendant who we all knew as "Boots," and me. Boots was well-liked and well-known by everyone who frequented the men's room, and he had a reputation for being friendly, polite, and very talkative. He could remember the name of everybody who visited his domain, and soon, everybody knew his name too.

It was his good service and friendly personality that enticed that gave him a good reputation, and usually enticed customers to give him generous tips. But none were as generous as Frank Sinatra was.

Sinatra's exceedingly generous tipping was no secret to anyone in New York City, to waiters, busboys, doormen, and everyone in between. He pulled out wads of cash, peeling off hundred-dollar bills, and handing them out with glee. And every time Sinatra entered the men's room, Boots's face would light up. He'd go through his routine, offering his best service, chatting a mile a minute, longing for that generous Sinatra tip.

I was always there when that happened because I often followed Frank to the bathroom to act as a security guard, preventing nosy fans from getting in his face. Every time Frank went into the men's room, many in the club would conveniently decide they needed to go there as well. It was like a spot hidden away from the pomp and circumstance, and the rules of civility that permeated the rest of the club. Once in the bathroom, they felt they could get away with ignoring his privacy and tried striking up a conversation in order to brag about it the next day. So I always made sure to escort Frank there and close the door to make sure that nobody came in to bother him.

One night, Sinatra was sitting at Table 17 with baseball manager Leo Durocher, and when the two men needed to go to the bathroom, I escorted them there and waited by the door. I got a kick out of watching happy Boots preparing to serve his favorite customer, handing him a towel and making small talk. But when Frank reached into his pocket and pulled out a one-hundred-dollar bill, ready to tip Boots, Durocher intervened and blocked his hand.

"No, Frank, you've been taking care of bills all night. I'll take care of the tip," he said, and he then handed two dollars to a stunned Boots.

As we were walking out, I glanced back at Boots, and I saw him standing there frozen, still holding the two dollars in disbelief, his broad smile now gone, and his face turning red. I escorted Frank and Durocher to their table, and when I was back at my desk, Boots stormed out of the men's room mad as hell, fuming.

"Dino, did you see what that motherfucker Durocher did to me, man? He cut me off $98 dollars, man, that son of a bitch. He cut me off $98 dollars, man."

I couldn't blame him. Back in the '70s, $100 was like a week's pay for some people. But I managed to calm him down a little by reminding him that Sinatra was a regular, and that there would be plenty of other opportunities, and finally, Boots returned to the men's room shaking his head, still mad.

Jimmy was at his usual spot at the bar, noticed the commotion with Boots, and came over to see what had happened. As I was telling him the story, I could see his mischievous side starting to come out. Jimmy lived for things like this, and he always knew how to elicit a good laugh. He found this story to be very funny, and he took it back to the bar to entertain his pals.

The story didn't end there. After that night, whenever Jimmy thought it was the right time for some laughs, he would invite Boots at the bar for a drink and get him rattled all over again. "Hey, Boots, tell us what happened with Sinatra and Durocher."

And Boots would explode. You would think it was the night of the incident all over again.

"Jimmy, man, why do you have to remind me of that, man?" he would say, his voice rising near falsetto. "That motherfucker Durocher, he cost me $98, man."

Then he would walk away mad, mumbling to himself and leaving behind a roar of laughter. Meanwhile, Boots knew that he had now entered Jimmy's inner circle at the bar—that meant that he got more tips. And so, he'd happily oblige them by returning to tell the story for some laughs every time Jimmy called him over.

As those bar hoppers traveled from bar to bar, they took that joke along with them, spreading the word of Boots's lost tips, and the long nights of laughter that Jimmy would stir up by getting Boots riled up again. Before long, this became one of the funniest stories in New York City, and Boots's name and colorful personality became somewhat known. There were even some people who had never been at the place who would stop by to meet and talk to Boots.

But the story wasn't over yet, continuing the next time Frank came in, this time with Jackie Kennedy, one of their very rare public appearances together, and at one point, he started toward the men's room and, as always, I followed him there. I watched Boots, eager as ever, nervously fidgeting around and moving every knickknack on the counter. As he finally picked up a towel and handed it to Frank, I could see a sense of happiness and relief on his face, knowing there was no one around to deny him his $100 bill.

"Thank you, Boots," he said, palming him the tip.

I escorted Frank back to Table 17, and when I returned back to the desk, there was Boots, once again in a tizzy.

"Dino!" he said. "Sinatra, he made a mistake."

"What now, Boots?" I asked.

"He gave me two hundred instead of one," he said. "What do I do? Should I give it back?"

I have to admit, I wasn't quite sure how to handle that, and I needed some time, so I told Boots to relax and to let me think about. I wasn't sure if it was even worth bringing up to Frank, and while I was trying to figure this out, Sinatra and Jackie went to leave. As usual, I escorted them outside to his limo. We said good night, and as he was getting into the limo, I decided to bring it up. "Boots thinks you made a mistake," I said.

But he waved me off. "I know about that. Just tell Boots I don't make mistakes," he said.

Even after Boots got his lost tip, the story never stopped. It was told at the bar for years to come. And about fifteen years later, when Jimmy Weston died, the story appeared again, this time in his *New York Times* obituary column.

CHAPTER 29

The Lady and the Chair

In the span of our twenty years in business, every day yielded new and interesting stories, each filled with twists and turns that I never expected, and this is one of many stories that I will always remember because it showed me the extreme measures a diehard fan is willing to take to meet their heroes, and what the people who they love will do to help them get there. It's a story I call the Lady and the Chair.

By now, we had gained a reputation as an oasis of sorts, a watering hole where the upper echelon of society came to unwind alongside the everyday New York men and women. It was common to see tables filled with people, quietly stretching their necks to try and catch a glimpse of the celebrities that were there, especially Sinatra.

Most of the celebrities came to unwind and hoped for some degree of privacy, and so we created some strict rules to protect them. For instance, we created a "no picture" rule inside the club in order to keep the paparazzi out. Another strict rule was a dress code that discouraged unruly behavior and ensured we maintained an atmosphere of class. From the beginning, people liked our system, and soon the place became its own ecosystem.

Everybody started coming in sharp and dapper, like they were competing to win an award for best dressed. And I took great pride in my ability to keep our rules enforced, to navigate that complex social code, and to be the crucial link between the stars and all the others who wanted to be part of it. I could speak both languages: the language of the common customer and the celebrity language. I understood the common people because I was a common man, and at Jimmy Weston's, I spent every single night mingling among the celebrities and came to call them my friends. I had one foot in each world—and I loved every minute of it.

But the world at Jimmy Weston's revolved around Frank Sinatra. He was the "king of the jungle," so to speak.

Every time, when he got up to leave, I would escort him outside to his limo and say good night, knowing that inside, his fans, especially women, were swarming Table 17 for souvenirs. They would take the ashtray, even with cigarette butts, or the glass he was drinking from. This was a usual thing, and it always added to the mystique of the place.

But one night, when I came back inside, I was surprised by a beautiful woman in her mid-thirties, waiting for me by my desk and hugging a chair tight into her chest. There was a guy standing next to her who seemed a bit uncomfortable, in direct contrast to her confident nature. To me, it was an awkward situation, and it started to attract curious onlookers. I didn't know what this was all about, but certainly I had to find out, and I hurried my steps toward them. But before I could even ask a question, the woman looked at me and asked one of her own. "How much?" she asked determinedly.

"What are you talking about?" I said.

"How much for this, the chair?"

"Ma'am, we don't sell chairs here," I said, chuckling in disbelief.

"Frank Sinatra sat in this chair, and I want to buy it," she said, her voice getting more demanding, her eyes widening and showing no signs of giving up.

The guy standing impatiently next to her pulled out a roll of cash and started to count bills. "Please," he said, "please sell it to her. I have to live with her."

Now I was amused. "What are you going to do with that chair?" I asked her.

"I'm going to put it in my living room, and nobody is going to sit on it ever again."

I looked at the woman, hugging this chair like it was already hers, and it became clear to me that she would never leave without it. I also realized that she was the boss, and I decided to tease them a little. "Five hundred dollars," I said in a serious tone, expecting the guy to panic or shove his money back into his pocket and tell the woman to drop the chair and leave. Or I thought maybe he'd try to haggle, come back with a lower price, and see who would give up first.

But to my surprise, he didn't flinch at all. Instead, he continued counting out the money as she watched him, smiling and pleased. I took a mental snapshot of the scene, thinking that I'd tell Frank about it the next time I'd see him, and I've never forgotten it. It was one of those vivid images of my Jimmy Weston's nights that often resurface.

I was impressed by her obsession and her devotion to Frank's chair but also was impressed by the guy's devotion to her. I also realized that I was dealing with a woman who always got what she wanted and a guy who would do anything for her no matter how badly I teased them. In the end, she'd always win.

"Put your money away," I told him. But he kept on counting, maybe to show me that he was willing to pay that exorbitant price for the chair. So then I told the woman to keep to keep the chair, compliments of Frank Sinatra.

Immediately, she thrust the chair into the guy's arms and threw her arms around me, shouting. "Thank you. I love you. Thank you," she kept going, kissing me and hugging me until finally, the guy cleared his throat to get back her attention.

"I'm still here, holding your chair," he complained.

We all laughed and introduced ourselves. Her name was Barbara and his name was Leonard, and they stayed talking with me like we were good friends of many years. They kept coming very often after that, hoping each night to see Barbara's favorite singer. And after many visits, finally, they hit the jackpot.

It was sometime later, shortly after Sinatra married Barbara Marx, and he came in with her and a big party including Gregory Peck and his wife, Veronica, Kirk Douglas and his wife, the comedian Don Rickles, and many others. The group was a bit more raucous and filled with laughter than usual, perhaps egged on by Rickles, who hadn't stopped with his harsh, roasting jokes since they walked in. It was a special treat for everyone in the place, seeing a parade

...rstars coming in, especially so loose and relaxed in a cloud ...aughter, and I could see that Barbara and Leonard could barely ...tand still.

Sometime later, Sinatra got up to go to the men's room. As I always did, I escorted him there to ensure that no crazed fans followed him in. I told him the story of the lady and the chair, and Frank was very much amused, especially when I told him that the couple happened to be there that night.

"Really?" he said enthusiastically. "Take me to them, but don't tell it to Rickles. He won't show them any mercy."

As we walked toward Barbara and Leonard's table, I could see their shocked expressions as they both stood up. But Frank, gracious as always, told them to relax and sat down with them.

"I heard you are collecting my chairs," he told Barbara.

They laughed, and then Barbara, smooth and confident as ever, was ready to ask for more. "I'd like to collect your autograph too," she told him.

Frank took out a pen. "What's your name, dear?"

"It's Barbara."

He jumped at the opportunity so quickly it almost seemed rehearsed. "Barbara?" Then he raised his voice over to the table where his new wife, Barbara, was sitting. "Barbara!" he yelled. "That's a marvelous name. It's the most beautiful name in the world. You know, I'm married to a beautiful gal with that sweet name, Barbara?"

Meanwhile, his new wife, Barbara, was now listening, along with the others.

"I know. She is a beautiful lady, and we're wishing you both the very best," she replied.

"Thank you, sweetheart," Frank said.

Then he put the pen to paper, ready to sign, and looked up to her. "Barbara, huh?" he asked again.

"Yes," Barbara said.

"Spell it," Frank asked her seriously.

That brought a loud laughter from everyone who was listening, especially his wife, Barbara. Then Don Rickles offered his objections. "Hey, hey, I'm supposed to be the comedian here," he said.

"I don't hear anyone laughing at your jokes," Sinatra zinged back.

When the laughter quieted down some, Barbara had come in prepared. She pulled out a little camera from her pocketbook and asked Frank if she could take a picture with him.

"There are rules here," he told her. Then he pointed at me. "You have to ask the skipper."

"It's up to you," I said.

"This is your house, pal. Why is it up to me?"

"If you're okay with it, I'm okay with it," I said. And they took the picture.

The rest of the night was filled with more grateful kisses from Barbara, more throat-clearing from Leonard, and lots more laughs all around.

The truth here is Frank did not have to ask my permission to take a picture. He could do whatever he wanted—he was Frank Sinatra. But that's the kind of guy Sinatra was. He would respect your rules as long as you respected his. And for my part, it was those moments that I reveled in the most, where I was in control of the night, orchestrating complex scenes like a theater director, to give the stars their nights of fun and the ordinary folks the memories they'd never forget.

CHAPTER 30

Christmas with Frank in Harlem

This is one of my stories that reveal the other side of Sinatra's complicated, multi-faceted personality. He was known by many as a hot-tempered tough guy, who never backed off from a fight; some columnists and enemies even connected him to the mafia. But I got to also know his soft, caring, and sensitive side, that he liked to keep private and only a few, outside of his family, or immediate friends ever got to see.

I was fortunate enough to see this side of him all the time, but never more so than on one night around Christmas time when the place was packed with a lively crowd that seemed poised to stay deep into the night, enjoying Tommy's smooth renditions of classic Christmas carols. Outside, thick sheets of snow were falling, injecting more seasonal spirit into the warm energy that permeated the room. And around midnight, Frank Sinatra walked in with his best friend and trusted companion, Jilly Rizzo.

This was not a surprise to me. My friend, Dorothy Uhlemann, Sinatra's personal secretary, told me ahead of time, as she always did, that "Mr. S." was in town for a few days, and I was expecting him to stop by as usual before calling it a night at his apartment at the Waldorf Towers just three blocks away.

After warm greetings and bear hugs, I escorted them to Table 17, and after a few drinks, at about 2:30 a.m., Frank called me over. "Hey, Greek," he said, "you got that old Chevy outside?"

"Yes, it's outside," I told him.

They both stood up; Frank peeled off a couple hundred dollars bills from his wad of cash and gave it to the waiter.

"Greek, you just got yourself drafted," he said. "Let's go."

I had no idea where we were going, but I knew I would be gone for a while, and I asked George Pappas, our captain, to take charge as me, Frank, and Jilly walked out to where Sinatra's limo was waiting. He told the driver to wait there, and we all piled into my five-year-old Chevy Impala. It was a bitter cold night, and the snow was still coming down heavily. But the weather hardly impeded driving in New York City, where the steam emanating from the subway grates kept the asphalt warm, melting the snow.

"Where we are going?" I asked.

"Uptown, to Patsy's Pizzeria," Jilly said.

We were traveling on Park Avenue when suddenly, Sinatra asked me to stop and pull over. When I brought my now famous limo near the sidewalk and stopped, Frank got out of the car, looking up to the sky with an expression of wonder and a smile on his face.

"Look at this. Isn't this marvelous?" he said, all excited.

Anxious to see what Frank was marveling at, Jilly and I got out of the car and joined him on the sidewalk. The snow was coming down steadily, and there was not a soul on the streets, which created a bewitching sense of privacy and peace that was virtually nonexistent on a normal New York City day or night. It was just us three, standing there, looking up into the sky with awe, like three children on Christmas morning, mulling over the mystery of how our presents appeared beneath the tree.

Big fat snowflakes, millions of them, were coming down, dancing between the skyscrapers, illuminated by the lights of the buildings. It was really a breathtaking sight, and all three of us were mystified, Frank especially. He had a deep appreciation for powerful, captivating imagery. Besides singing and acting, Sinatra also had a huge appetite for painting, drawing, and photography, often inspired by such scenes. In fact, we had two blown-up pictures that he had taken of the famous Muhammad Ali and Joe Frazier fight at Madison Square Garden on display at Jimmy Weston's.

Clearly, that night left an impression on Frank's artistic mind. A good friend of mine, Ana Cruz, Sinatra's traveling coordinator and a visitor to his Palm Springs home, years later, told me that she saw a painting in Sinatra's home of three guys standing on a New York City sidewalk, staring up into the snow.

We stood out there, admiring Mother Nature's show for some time. I don't know how long we were there exactly; it's easy to get lost in such things, but after we were coated with snow, we got back into my car and kept driving until we reached Harlem and eventually made a beeline for 1st Avenue, between 117th and 118th streets, to Patsy's Pizzeria.

I had never been there before, and as we arrived, I realized that Frank had asked me to take the Chevy because it wasn't a good idea to go there in a limo in the wee hours. I parked the car in front of the place and we went in. The restaurant was empty, and we were greeted by Carmela, the owner. She was a cheery, 150 percent amazing Italian woman whose welcoming demeanor made that pizzeria feel like her family's dining room. When she saw Frank, she rushed to him with open arms and a wide smile. "Frankie, sweetheart, it's so good to see you again," she said.

She put her arms around him and gave him a strong bear hug, and when she pulled away, Frank's dark coat was powdered white with the flour from Carmela's apron. Embarrassed, she started muttering quickly in Italian, almost like she was cursing at herself while trying to brush off the mess she made.

"Ah don't worry about that, babe. Just make us your delicious pizza," he told her.

She hurried away and soon came back with a whole pizza, and as we started to eat, Frank looked out the window and noticed these two homeless guys staring in at us. We saw them also; they were shivering from the cold and hunger. Frank waved them in and called out to Carmela, ordering pizza for them. But then, more guys showed up, and soon, the place was filled with Sinatra's impromptu and ravenous guests, and he ordered pizza for all of them.

While Jilly and I finished our slices, we noticed that Sinatra had only taken one bite of his. With teary eyes, he was watching those poor hungry guys gobbling down the hot, steaming slices as fast they could. And that got Jilly's attention because he knew that Sinatra was an emotional man, and often, his emotions manifested into heavy drinking.

I remember one late night, a few weeks after the death of actor Yul Brynner, Frank's good friend and golf buddy. Frank and Jilly were there at Jimmy Weston's, and Frank fell into a drinking binge. Jilly yanked the drink out of Frank's hand, angrily spilling it on the table. I had expected to see Frank react violently, but he didn't. I learned then that Jilly was the only person who could do such a thing to Frank Sinatra because instead of getting angry, Frank took Jilly's strong suggestion to call it a night and get some sleep.

Now, in Patsy's Pizzeria, as Frank was getting emotional, Jilly tried to divert his attentions elsewhere.

"You see, Frank," he said, "you aren't as famous as you think you are. No one recognized you here."

"If you were as hungry and cold as they are, you wouldn't recognize me either," Frank snapped back, his eyes getting redder and waterier.

"Are you going to eat your pizza, or should we go now?" Jilly asked.

Frank stood up, pulled out his wad of hundreds, and handed the whole thing over to Carmela, without even counting.

"What the hell, it's Christmas," he said. "Keep the pizza coming through Christmas, darling. I'll send you some more. And keep everything under wraps."

"This is more than enough, sweetheart. Have a Merry Christmas and don't worry. I'll take care of it," she told him. Then she took off her apron to hug him again, and as we started walking toward the door, those two guys who came in first walked over and stepped in front of him.

"Thank you, Mr. Sinatra, and have a Merry Christmas," they told him.

"Come back here tomorrow. There will be more hot pizza for you. Stay off the junk, and have a Merry Christmas," he told them.

As we were getting into the car, others came out waving to us, and shouting out "Thank you, Mr. Sinatra, and have a Merry Christmas!"

While driving back, Frank was very quiet and deep in thought, unresponsive to all of our attempts to make conversation. But after remaining quiet for most of the ride, finally, Frank asked one question: "Have you ever been cold and hungry?"

"I have," I told him.

But the rest of the way back to Jimmy Weston's, we sat in silence. When we arrived, I pulled in front of the place, and that's when he broke his silence again.

"Thanks for the ride, Greek," he said before rushing to get into his limo with Jilly following him.

So many Christmases have passed since then, but I will always remember that special one. And life went on with so many more sweet memories like this, and I was always thankful that I was lucky enough to be a part of them.

CHAPTER 31

The Feud

I'll always remember the day that Jimmy Weston's brought two adversaries together, just when it seemed they would never get along.

At the time, Frank Sinatra's popularity was growing rapidly at the national and international levels. He was traveling and performing all over the world, entertaining millions and socializing with presidents, prime ministers, and more.

But for many tabloid columnists, Frank's fast rising profile presented an opportunity for a free ride to fame. Those writers were always looking to print something negative or controversial about Frank, knowing that, with his hot temper, he would react strongly and publicly, unwittingly boosting their popularity.

One of them was a *New York Daily News* gossip columnist named Liz Smith who frequently wrote columns about Frank that rubbed him the wrong way. Frank would react with some classy words of his own, creating a long-running war between them that often spilled out into public view. Unintentionally, Sinatra was doing Liz a favor, as all the publicity drove more people to read Smith's columns and learn more gossip about the megastar.

At Jimmy Weston's, every single night carried the potential for something special to happen. It was a stage where special moments in entertainment history often played out before our customers. Sometimes, they'd happen behind the scenes, but they'd captivate nonetheless, and I was privileged to peek backstage for many historic moments. As it would turn out, our club would become a little-known focal point in Sinatra's feud with Liz Smith. It was there where the two of them arrived at a truce.

We had this private alcove next to the bar, which was off to the left when you first walked in. It could comfortably fit eight people; it was soundproof with redwood paneling all around, and it was available by request to business people who wanted to discuss private affairs. Joe Marino, our house bookie, for instance, would settle bets there with his clients.

One night, Frank called me over and told me to keep the alcove available for him for the next evening at six thirty. It was kind of an unusual request from Sinatra, especially because of the time. He usually wouldn't arrive at the place until around midnight or later.

"Make sure I get privacy," he said.

I knew what that meant: I wouldn't tell anybody that Frank would be there, not even Jimmy.

Every evening at 5:00 p.m. and after, the happy hour would start, and the place was crowded and noisy. The next evening at six twenty, when happy hour was going on in full swing, Sinatra walked in alone. I discreetly escorted him through the crowded cocktail lounge over to the alcove. I had no idea what this was about until Frank told me that, soon, Liz Smith would be coming in and that I should bring her there.

I knew I had heard him correctly, but I couldn't quite believe that he was meeting with Liz Smith, and so I had to double-check.

"Liz Smith?" I asked, awestruck.

"Yes, that big-mouthed broad," he assured me.

I smiled to myself, and as I walked back to my desk to wait for Liz Smith to arrive, I had only one thought: "This is going to be a fun night."

A few minutes later, Smith came in, alone. I had never met her, but I recognized her from pictures in her column and politely greeted her. She was polite and returned the greeting and told me that Mr. Sinatra was expecting her, so I escorted her through the crowd to the alcove and stood by the entrance to make sure that no one came near.

Suddenly, the happy hour chatter and laughter immediately stopped, and everyone's total attentions were riveted toward the alcove with disbelief. There was no more laughter or loud conversation, only a few, hushed, whispered exchanges. Even the bartenders found themselves standing still, staring at the alcove just like all the others, anxious to hear or see something. It was like being in the courtroom of a high-profile trial, waiting for the jury to deliver its verdict. Everyone expected that this long and nasty feud would boil over into something much larger after so many years of tension, like a volcanic explosion bursting from the alcove.

But nothing like that happened. It was quiet for about a half hour until Liz came out, walking quickly, and left. Not long after, Frank came out, and as I was escorting him through the crowd, he noticed that everyone was standing still and quiet, looking at him, stunned.

He suddenly broke away from me and squeezed himself through the crowd. I wasn't surprised; with Frank, it was impossible to predict what he was going to do next, and he rarely turned down an opportunity to surprise rubbernecking fans. Everybody made a path for him to walk through until he reached the middle of the floor and stopped. He then extended his hands out to everybody. "Sorry to disappoint you, folks," he said. "I just wasn't in a fighting mood tonight."

The silence that had now captivated the whole place broke into loud laughter and thunderous applause. I could see the afterglow on his face; it was the same that I had seen many times when he was on stage performing to adoring fans.

"Hey, Joe, Bobby, drinks for everybody," he told the bartenders.

Then he stood there, talking and shaking hands until I escorted him to Table 17, and when we got there, he gave me two one hundred-dollar bills. "Give these to the guys behind the bar and bring me the bar check," he told me.

And that was it. The happy hour resumed, and the many years of vicious feuding between Sinatra and Smith ended in thirty minutes at Jimmy Weston's alcove.

Soon, just as the Boots's story had spread fast throughout the city, this one spread too, but much faster, and I began facing a constant line of questions. People would always come up to me and ask me what happened. "What did you hear in the alcove? What did they say to each other?"

The truth was, I had no idea. I couldn't hear anything that they talked about. And honestly, even if I had heard, I wouldn't have told anyone.

But still, the story of their feud lived on and kept spreading like a wildfire around New York City, even as the columns stopped and the insults subsided, and I became the target of questions to all who came to hear my side.

One late night, Jimmy and I were bullshitting with four young wannabe type of guys at the bar. They were newcomers on the scene, sporting heavy gold chains and pinky rings, and like everyone else, they wanted to hear stories about Sinatra. They must have heard what had happened, and they kept pressing me to tell them what Frank had said to Liz Smith that made her stop the nasty gossip columns. I kept telling them the truth, which was that I didn't know, but they kept insisting.

Finally, I figured out a way to end the conversation. "I am going to say this to you only," I told them, and immediately, I got their full attention. Then I got very serious and leaned in, channeling Marlon Brando's Don Corleone from *The Godfather*.

"Frank made her an offer she couldn't refuse."

I could tell these guys loved what they heard and became very amused and satisfied.

"Frank is the man," one barked out.

"I'll drink to that," I said, raising my glass.

We made a toast, and after more drinks, it became obvious that their night was now made, and they kept looking over at the alcove where everything went down. I bought them a round, and later at closing time, we called it a night on a high note. After that, they started coming back often, and to impress their girlfriends, they'd always ask to sit at the alcove so they could tell the story.

CHAPTER 32

Table 17—Where Everything Happened

Liz Smith wasn't the only tabloid columnist who picked fights with Sinatra, and certainly not the only one who found fame by feuding with him. Others, like frustrated actor-turned-columnist Rex Reed, along with Rona Barrett and cartoonist Gary Trudeau, knew that making Sinatra angry was an easy way to get their names known because of his explosive reactions.

But none of those feuds created more buzz and generated more national headlines and controversy than one that I got to be a part of. It all started in Washington during President Richard Nixon's inauguration, after the *Washington Post* columnist Maxine Cheshire really got under Sinatra's skin by writing numerous bad things about him in her columns and insinuating that he had ties to the mafia.

It was at that time when one evening, during a social event in Washington, and when Sinatra walked in with Jilly Rizzo, he saw Maxine standing there holding a cocktail drink, his temper immediately rose like a steaming teakettle ready to boil over. Immediately, he figured out what he wanted to do, and he needed two-dollar bills for his plan, but he never carried any small bills, so he borrowed two dollars from Jilly without offering an explanation. Then he stormed over to Maxine and shoved the two dollars into her glass.

"Here, you've been laying down for two dollars all your life," he told her, loud and clear, shocking everyone in the room.

There were many other columnists and paparazzi covering the event, so the story was picked up quickly and printed in papers all over the country, prompting media outrage and calls for Sinatra to apologize, which he never did. He was not one to back down from a fight, especially when he believed he was right, and the issue lingered in the press for a long time.

A few months later, he was performing a concert in New York City at Carnegie Hall. I had come to the show with my family, expecting a fun, easygoing night of wonderful music and great company. The opening act was a comedian, I think his name was Tom Dresden, and in between sets, there was a fifteen-minute intermission, at which point my family and I were invited backstage for a quick drink and chat with Frank.

It was fifteen minutes packed with warm greetings, well wishes, and as many laughs as one could pack in such a short time, and Sinatra seemed calm and relaxed. Eventually, the lights flicked on and off, signaling that it was show time and that we needed to return to our seats. But before we left, the ever-present Jilly Rizzo came over to talk to Frank.

"Frank," he said, "don't mention anything tonight about that broad in Washington. You gave her enough publicity already."

"So you're telling me that I should apologize to her?" Frank snapped back, and Jilly walked away.

We returned to our seats, and Frank walked onstage to a standing ovation. He sang three or four songs and energized the crowd. Then he took a drink off the piano behind him, held it up to the audience, and began to make a toast. "Thank you very much, ladies and gentlemen. I am so happy to be back here at the Big Apple, singing for a live audience like you. You are the best audience, and I wish you all a long healthy life of a hundred fifty years and more, but that the last voice you hear will be mine. Salute."

He raised his drink and took a swallow, and the crowd broke into laughter and applause, then he continued, with the full attention of everyone in the audience, "By now, I am sure that you all heard what happened a few months ago in Washington with me and this so-called newspaper woman, whose name I will not mention."

Jilly was sitting next to me, and I could hear him murmuring. "Here we go again…" as Frank continued.

"She wrote some very nasty things about me, and when I met her at a cocktail party, I put two dollars in her glass and called her a two-bit whore, and now, ladies and gentlemen, publicly, I want to apologize to her because she is not a two-bit whore… She is one-bit whore…"

Immediately, Carnegie Hall's auditorium, filled with 2,800 people, burst into a thunderous standing ovation that seemed to last forever, ending only when Frank asked the crowd to stop and sit down, but their enthusiasm never waned. He continued on with the show, receiving thunderous applause, song after song.

After the concert, I sent my family home, and I returned to Jimmy Weston's, knowing that Frank, as always, would stop by for a nightcap before retreating to his hotel for the night. At that time, everybody knew that when Sinatra was in town, he can always be found at Jimmy Weston's, and by the time I got there, a huge crowd had already gathered outside, waiting for his arrival. Inside, the place was packed wall-to-wall with only Table 17 kept reserved for Frank.

Finally, at about 4:00 a.m., after making some other stops around the city, Sinatra arrived with Jilly. By this time the place had emptied out, with those who had hoped to see him giving up and heading home disappointed.

So Jimmy and I joined them at Table 17 to close out the evening, and there, the saga continued as we kept talking about the long standing ovation Frank had received at Carnegie Hall, awed at how well his comments had been received by his loyal crowd.

"I've had many long-standing ovations before, but I've never had one for calling someone a two-bit whore," he said.

"I don't know about that, Francis," said Jimmy, who was always quick with a joke.

"I think you *still* offered her too much money," and Jilly followed up with another one.

"*Yia*, he is pretty generous with my money."

Today, as I recall these moments, what stands out most is how much fun it was to be around such a witty group of characters, who all had incredible senses of humor. Every day with them was like an Abbott and Costello skit; they were funny, spontaneous, sharp, and unpredictable. Before you knew it, you could be in the middle of an improvised bit, or a practical joke, or simply a series of classic one-liners. You never knew what they'd come up with next.

And all the best always happened there at Table 17. For me, being there with them felt like having a ticket to the most unforgettable show in town. I will always remember the time when Jimmy was looking to hire a houseboy for his new, big, seaside house in Spring Lake, New Jersey, and Sinatra offered to send him one of his own.

It all started when Jimmy decided to open another Jimmy Weston's club in Spring Lake, New Jersey—a beautiful resort community that had become a getaway heaven for all the Irish, rich and famous, who were our best drinking customers. For most of the year, they filled our club night after night, putting away drinks faster than the waiters could bring them. But every summer we would lose them to their heavenly retreat in Spring Lake, and it became a noticeable hole in our business. So Jimmy embarked on opening another Jimmy Weston's out there, aiming to follow our best customers on their seasonal migration.

While he was preparing the project, he saw a huge house for sale near a beach that he loved, and he couldn't resist buying it. He, too, would settle there for the summer with his wife, Karen, and his two daughters, Jennifer and Jamie, inviting friends from the city to visit and stay in his guesthouse.

However, the house was so big that it needed "a houseboy" to help maintain and work on it, but Jimmy had no luck finding anyone in Spring Lake. He eventually brought on a guy named Ming from New York City, but things didn't work out well, and Jimmy was getting upset. So it was one of those late nights we were sitting with Frank and Jilly at Table 17, drinking and unwinding as usual, and at one point Frank asked Jimmy when he would be opening the other joint in Spring Lake.

"In a couple weeks we should have the grand opening, but I shouldn't have bought that big house," Jimmy complained.

"What's wrong with the house?" Sinatra asked.

"It's too big, Frank, and I can't find a good houseboy to help out."

Everyone in Sinatra's inner circle knew he never hesitated to help out a friend in need. But at the same time, he was known as a big practical joker, always looking for an angle to pull a funny prank on people he really liked for big laughs. And so, seeing Jimmy's situation as an opportunity for one of his famous gags, he jumped at the chance, and offered some help. "Hey, Cop," Frank said, using his usual nickname for Jimmy. "I have someone who worked for me for years. I'm not using him much now, but I am keeping him on payroll because he has been very good and very loyal. I'll send him to see you."

Jimmy's face lit up; he considered his problem solved. He thanked Frank for his offer, and the night ended with more drinks and happy conversations.

A couple nights later, around closing time, Sammy Davis Jr. showed up.

For those younger readers unfamiliar with Sammy Davis Jr., he was a tiny black guy with tons of talent and a great voice that had propelled him onto the national stage, making him a household name. He was one of Sinatra's best friends and a member of his "Rat Pack," which consisted only of Sinatra's inner circle, a group of top-tier performers. Frank and Sammy were particularly close; they had appeared in movies together and performed alongside each other in many concerts across the country.

As always, we welcomed Sammy, and we sat with him at Table 17, casually talking and having drinks, when suddenly Sammy leaned in and took a more serious posture with Jimmy, like he was ready to talk business.

"Frank asked me to come and talk to you about helping you out in Spring Lake," he told Jimmy with a straight face.

I knew Jimmy for many years. I'd seen him handle drunks at the bar, effortlessly socialize with the most powerful people in the city, and build our business from a dream to a reality. He was always a calm and collected smooth talker who could work his way out of any situation easily.

But now, as I looked at him, I could see he was at a loss for words. He stammered, trying to find the best way to respond, looking toward me like a lost puppy dog asking for help.

Honestly, I was shocked at Sammy's request as well, but it was kind of fun seeing Jimmy, for the first time ever, become numb and speechless. Meanwhile, Sammy just kept looking at him, waiting for him to say something. The whole thing probably lasted only a few seconds, but it felt like an hour, with Jimmy's bewilderment becoming increasingly noticeable and uncomfortable. I tried hard not to laugh, and I asked the waiter to bring us another round, just to break the ice.

Finally, after twisting on his chair, Jimmy cleared his throat, and somehow found the courage to talk. "Sam, there must be some misunderstanding here. Maybe it was my fault. Maybe I didn't explain to Frank that... But you see, Sammy, this job is not for you," he said.

That set Sammy off. "Man, what the hell do you mean this job is not for me? I've been doing this since I was eight years old, man," he said.

It became a very difficult situation for both Jimmy and me. After all, we were facing a superstar and Sinatra's dear friend who was clearly insulted. Jimmy looked to me as we both tried to find the right words. But our silences gave Sammy the suspicion that something crazy was going on.

"All right, you guys, just give it to me straight. I want to know what the hell is going on here," he demanded.

Jimmy then got the courage to set the record straight. "Sam, Frank and I, we were talking about hiring a houseboy that I need for my house over at Spring Lake."

Sammy went on a rampage. "That son of a bitch, he did it to me again," he yielded. "And I fell for it. He told me to come and talk to you about singing a few songs and kick off the grand opening of your new place. He must be laughing his ass off right now knowing that I really bought it, and I'm here... That cat is out of control, man..."

When he calmed down some, he asked us to side with him and tell Sinatra that he never showed up. But Sinatra must have timed everything perfectly, because just then, he walked in with Jilly, and as soon as he saw us sitting with Sammy, he knew that his prank had come to life. He put on a serious face, took a napkin from a table, and placed it on Sammy's arm, and in a somewhat commanding voice, told him, "Keep practicing, Sammy, go and get us another round here."

That set off Sammy again, sending some classic remarks to Frank, but it was so obvious; it all was for fun and love for each other.

After more laughs and zings, the two embraced, hugged, and the night continued on with fun till wee hours. These were two of the most talented men of their generation, and it was so obvious that they had a deep love and respect for each other.

I remember those days well when people could zing each other for fun and not be offended. There was another late night with a group of us that included Sammy Davis Jr. and an elderly Jewish guy named Toots Shor. He was the senior member of the group, a pre-Jimmy Weston's famous restaurateur with a great sense of humor who loved to hang out with us and exchange stories and fun.

A few years earlier, Sammy Davis Jr. had married a beautiful Jewish girl named May Britt and had converted his religion to Judaism. At that time, marriages between black and white people were rare and nonexistent in the Deep South where segregation was still very strong, even to the point where black people were forced to sit in the rear of a bus.

So that night, Toots decided to pull a joke on Sammy by giving him advice.

"You know, Sammy," he told him, "being a Jew now still is not going to make any difference. When you ever visit the Deep South, be careful. To them you are still black."

"I just returned from touring the South," Sammy said. "One day I got on a bus and set in the front, and when the bus driver ordered me to go and sit in the rear of the bus, I protested. 'But I am a Jew now,' I told him."

"'Then get the hell out of the bus,' the driver demanded."

We all broke into hysterical laughter.

As I said before, those were the carefree good days when one could tell any joke, everybody laughed, and no one got offended. Many times, I was a target of such jokes; born in Greece, I was called the Greasy Greek. We called the Italians Gunnies. We all had fun laughing together, living life. To its fullest.

CHAPTER 33

The Wise Guys and Their Shadows

Right after we opened the place, I found myself dealing with the glitzy celebrity world, the political elite, and the world of ordinary New Yorkers. It was a fascinating balancing act that made my job interesting and glamorous. Soon, however, I also had to deal with the wise guys and New York's mafia bosses, who took joy in being seen out in such places.

The first mob guys that I got to know came from the old-school; they liked to keep a low profile and not attract much attention, preferring to hide in plain sight, boasted only by their reputations instead of a flashy swagger. That mindset was embodied in guys like Aniello "Neil" Dellacroce, the underboss of the notorious Gambino family, and the boss of the up-and-coming mobster John Gotti.

The underboss was a low-key guy, and besides the FBI and the undercover cops who were always shadowing him, only a few of us actually knew who he was. For years, he came to Jimmy Weston's every Friday night with his girlfriend, Mary-Ann, and two other friends, who I got to know as Vinnie and Louie, Dellacroce's bodyguards. It was a routine for the waiters to set up their table with the needed ingredients for making wine spritzers: a ball of ice, a wine cooler with a bottle of Chablis, lemon peels, and a few bottles of club soda.

Dellacroce never spoke much about anything, and he rarely smiled. I could only see him cracking a crocodile grin whenever Tommy sang his favorite song, "Wise Guy." Otherwise, he sat in his chair, stone-faced, endlessly puffing his Tiparillos, and sipping on his spritzer as Vinnie and Louie lumbered next to him, keeping a watchful eye on things.

However, even Neil Dellacroce and his crew couldn't resist succumbing to that loose brotherly atmosphere that enveloped everyone at Jimmy Weston's, and over the years, they became a little more open with me. We'd exchange some friendly greetings and brief conversation when they entered, and during the night, as I'd be strolling around the dining room doing my usual rounds, and I'd always pass by their table to make sure everything was in order. I'd make eye contact with Dellacroce, who appreciated the attention and would nod his head in satisfaction, and I'd return back to my desk.

This went on for years, until one night, the waiter came over to tell me that Mr. Dellacroce wanted to see me. That struck me as odd because in all the years I'd known him, he never asked for me to come see him at his table, and on my way there, I was wondering what this could possibly be about.

When I arrived at their table, I noticed the stone-cold expressions on their faces, signaling to me that this would not be a pleasant conversation. I stood next to Dellacroce, and before I could say anything, he waved me closer and put his hand around my neck, bringing my head close to his. He planted his mouth close to my ear, and in a deep voice, he whispered, "Get the cement."

I was stunned. I knew I heard him clearly, but I had no idea what he meant, and to make sure there was no misunderstanding, I pulled away to try and clarify with him what it was exactly that he wanted.

"I am sorry, Mr. Neil. I don't understand," I told him.

"What? Am I talking Greek to you? I said get the cement," he said, firm and serious.

He looked at me with his cold eyes and without his crocodile grin. His tone was deep and sharp, like he was ordering one of his henchmen to kill somebody. Now, I looked over to Vinnie, Louie,

200

and Mary-Ann, believing that, certainly, after years of developing a friendly rapport, one of them would give me some kind of clue.

But they too were cold and still as stone, with a deadly expression on their faces, looking at me like they had never seen me before. Immediately, I realized that, whatever it was, it was certainly not a good situation for me to be involved with, and I was startled to see such cold expressions staring back at me from people who I had known for a long time. I stood there, momentarily thinking about how that must have been what it takes to carry out the dark deeds that the mafia was known for. You have to be capable of being cold and harsh to even the friendliest of faces, of being able to remove all sense of emotion and sympathy and take care of business. In any event, I could tell that something serious was going on here, and I feared that I would now be on the receiving end of one of those moments.

But what was it with the cement? I thought. *And what did I have to do with any of it?*

I assumed my maître d' position and politely responded, "I am sorry, but I don't have cement here. What for?"

"What for, you say?" he asked, looking at me very angry, like I had asked him a question that I should never have asked. Then he pointed to the ice bowl on the table where the ice had melted, leaving mostly water.

"Don't you see?" he said. "That son of a bitch is still floating. Tell your guys to use cement."

I looked at the ice bowl and noticed, with some relief, what he was referring to: a small bug was floating in the icy water, and before I could say something, he cracked that crocodile smile. "I got you, didn't I?" he said.

"Yes, you did. That's very funny...and I'll get my guys to use some cement," I said.

Immediately, Vinnie and Louie started laughing hard and moving their upper bodies back and forth. It truly reminded me of a scene from a gangster movie I had seen, where the mobsters belted a loud phony laugh simply to please their boss after he said something funny.

As I've said, pulling gags on each other was a big part of some nights. I remember well, for instance, how during Monday Night Football, the cocktail lounge was always packed with fans and gamblers, and whenever a critical play that would decide the fate of the game was about to transpire, like just as the ball was kicked into the air on a game-winning field goal attempt, Jimmy would turn the TV off. All the gamblers who were watching breathlessly to see if that field goal was going to make them winners or losers would erupt with boos while the rest of us would erupt with laughter.

Those pranks were part of the atmosphere of the place, and everyone expected them. Everyone was always on guard, trying to avoid being the target of a prankster's joke. But honestly, I had never expected any gag at all to come from a mafia underboss, especially one who always appeared so stone-faced and who made great efforts to keep a low profile. Maybe, it was the simple fact that he was a human too, eager to have fun like everyone else in the club, especially after spending so much time behind bars.

There were many other wise guys who made the place their prime watering hole, and I always had to deal with them, but I never did learn their real names. I got to know them only by their nicknames, like Frankie Chi-Chi, Mike Moose, Jimmy Hot-Hot, Vinnie the Umbrella, Anthony the Mechanic, and many others. They all got their nicknames from something they did in the past, or something that they were doing, like Anthony the Mechanic. Outside of his mafia work, he was a mechanic who was like the Pope for all the city's video game and juke box machines; they could only be operated with Anthony's blessings.

They'd all come in crisp suits, bringing their girlfriends, who'd be adorned in fur coats and jewelry. They'd order the most expensive wines, drinks, and food. They weren't a noisy or rowdy bunch, but they were different from Dellacroce, a little more sociable, a little flashier. They liked to be noticed while out dancing and drinking all night.

However, it was obvious to me, and to anyone paying attention, that these wise guys were all obsessed with Frank Sinatra. They would constantly watch him over at Table 17, studying his habits and trying to emulate him whenever they could, ordering his favorite drink, Jack Daniels, and trying to replicate his mannerisms.

For instance, Sinatra and I always greeted each other with a big hug, and soon, these guys would come in and say "Hey, Dino" before grabbing me and squeezing me with a big hard bear hug, so hard that I often felt like I needed to see the chiropractor. They'd even started to copy Sinatra's generous tipping habits, handing out hundred-dollar bills to those who served them. On some occasions, I'd get a generous tip if I let them sit at Table 17 when Sinatra wasn't in town. Sitting there seemed to make them feel like they were a part of his inner circle. It was good for our business, and we all loved getting their tips.

Over the years, rumors would spread, often playing out in the gossip columns, about Frank's relationship with the mafia. Even today, people who were there or who heard the stories will often come up to me and ask the same old question: "Hey, Dino, was Frank Sinatra with the mafia, as some people say?"

And I'm always happy to answer with something they never expect to hear: "It was the other way around. Frank wasn't with the mafia. The mafia was with him."

I tell them and I sit back to watch them wonder with their jaws hitting the floor.

Out of all the wise guys I got to know over the years, there was one who was drastically different from all the others. His name was Dennis. He was a young flamboyant guy who would come in with his crew of young men who called themselves The Purple Gang, originally the Westies, from Hell's Kitchen over on the west side on Tenth Avenue. Their reign of extortion, drugs, and murder made them the most feared gang New York ever had known. Even members of the mafia were afraid of them, aware of their reputation.

I had heard of the Westies but never knew much about them. However, I met them in very strange and dangerous circumstances. It happened one night when a group of six young guys in their thirties walked in, led by a tall guy. He was well-dressed, sharp in a pinstriped dark suit and a swagger. They all stormed past me as they entered, totally ignoring me, marching into the dining room, and seating themselves at Table 23, a big round table in the back that was the wise guys' preferred table because it had a clear view of the main entrance. I always kept a "Reserved" sign on it.

That was the only time that something like that had ever happened. Whether it was Frank Sinatra, Richard Nixon, George Steinbrenner, or just a regular customer, they all had the courtesy to stop by the desk until either me, Nick, or George would escort them to a table. Even the other members of the mafia did the same.

I had no idea who these arrogant guys were, and now, I was a little ticked off by the way they walked in like they owned the place. We had rules, and everyone knew how important those rules were to ensure that the place remained the harmonious oasis that it was reputed to be. Apparently, these guys didn't seem to understand that, or they didn't know it, so I had to let them know, and I walked over to their table.

"Fellows, this table is reserved," I told them as I pointed to the "Reserved" sign.

"Yeah, it's for us," said the tall guy sarcastically, seeming to be their leader.

"The next time, stop by the desk, and I'll give you a table," I told him, and I walked back to my desk.

Jimmy was at the bar, from where he was always watching what was going on by looking at the mirrors behind the bar's shelves, between the bottles. He had seen those guys coming in and came over to me.

"That's Dennis, from the Westies," he said, with a bit of warning in his voice. "Bend a little with him."

"I already did. But I won't show him my ass," I told Jimmy.

"Buy them a drink from me," Jimmy answered before heading back to the bar.

They were drinking champagne, and after a while, I followed Jimmy's instructions and took a bottle of Dom Perignon, went over to them, and placed the bottle on the table.

"This is from Jimmy Weston," I told them, looking at Dennis.

"And who the fuck is Jimmy Weston?" Dennis snapped, making the others giggle.

He had pushed the wrong button now, and I didn't care about what Jimmy wanted me to do, or who this guy was. I didn't care whether he was Dennis from the Westies or Neil Dellacroce. He had gone too far, and I wasn't going to let him bully me or Jimmy around.

I wasn't afraid. I had survived the reign of brutal communists in Greece and had since come so far, and I wasn't about to be intimidated. So I just treated him like he was any other jerk who didn't understand common courtesy and respect. I didn't hesitate and grabbed the bottle off the table. But as I turned to leave, I heard him say, "Where are you going with that?"

"If you don't know who Jimmy Weston is, then you shouldn't have this," I snapped back.

"I know Jimmy, and you better learn who I am," he said. "And put that bottle back on the table."

"Look, Dennis," I said, "I know who you are, and I will welcome you here, and as long as you respect my position and this place, we'll respect you and we're going to get along fine."

Dennis was a smart fellow, just like all the other mobsters. That's why they call them "wise guys." He knew what kind of a place Jimmy Weston's was, but he didn't quite know me, and I guess he had to find out. This is what the wise guys do. They may act tough, but the truth is, they never want to create any real trouble in a place where they hung out. Instead, they want to get to know everybody there and even make some friends.

"Sit down and have a drink with us," he said, telling the waiter to bring another glass. I sat with them, he poured some champagne, and we toasted each other though we were still strangers and clearly trying to figure each other out. It was my first interaction with Dennis and his crew, who continued to come often after that night.

To the general public, they may have seemed like any ordinary group of guys. But to the wise guys who knew him and his lethal reputation well, he was the notorious and dangerous Dennis, and they kept their distance from him. There were rumors that even the mob would commission Dennis and the Westies to carry out some of their more difficult killings. But ever since our talk, Dennis and his gang had become civil and friendly, just like any other group of guys unwinding after a long day of work. It took some time, but eventually, Dennis and I would grow to respect each other, becoming a little closer until years later, he would become my catalyst, ushering in a dark chapter that would bring new kinds of dangers.

Another wise guy who loved getting attention was the mafia chieftain John Gotti. He started coming in the later years, after his boss Dellacroce died, and after he arranged the killing of his new boss, Paul Castellano, and became the boss of the Gambino family.

Gotti was a real flamboyant guy in his forties, always sharply dressed in expensive suits, shiny shoes, and gaudy jewelry that made him stand out in a crowd and earned him the nickname "the Dapper Don."

He would always pull up in a big car and make an entrance filled with flair that caught everyone's attention. He was the antithesis of all the other wise guys. He lived in the spotlight, and he wanted everyone to know that he was the boss. That was a cardinal mafia rule that he broke and probably a reason for his downfall sometime later.

Often, he would come with his underboss, Sammy "the Bull" Gravano, an admitted killer of nineteen, including his brother-in-law. All night long, Sammy was scanning the surroundings, sipping on the same drink for hours, and never finishing it. Gotti, meanwhile, would be making sure that everybody knew who he was.

One night for instance, there was this couple celebrating their first wedding anniversary and Gotti told me to bring them a bottle of Dom Pérignon along with his best wishes. Rumors were that he did this sort of thing everywhere he went.

But while Jimmy Weston's attracted all sorts of wise guys, it never got a reputation as a mob hangout like other places did. That's because there was something about the place that attracted everybody, from Frank to Muhammad Ali to heroes like Buzz Aldrin and Neil Armstrong, New Yorkers from all walks of life. Even visitors from abroad would make sure to put it on their schedule to visit at least once. Not even the possibility of sitting next to the mafia guys could keep people away.

And of course, for every mobster who visited the place, there was another legendary cop keeping a watchful eye, like a shadow that was never too far away. Often, I could see an odd pairing of cops and robbers, undercover detectives sitting just a few feet away from the mafia lords like John Gotti and Aniello Dellacroce who they spent their days trying to bust. For me, it was kind of an adventure, being the gatekeeper for this unique mix of celebrities, politicians, wise guys, and undercover cops, all together in my circle.

I got to know a detective, Sergeant Joe Coffey, who became famous for taking a confession from the infamous "Son of Sam" killer, David Berkowitz. Coffey had also been known for arresting Gotti on several occasions.

Another tough cop who came there and who became a good friend was Richard "Bo" Dietl. He was known for going after New York's worst criminals. With 1,400 felony arrests and 75 medals and awards, he single-handedly broke the infamous case of a Harlem Catholic nun who had been raped and mutilated, and he earned national praise.

And there was an undercover cop named Sonny Grosso, Jimmy's ex-partner, who became best known as the lead detective of a case that was the inspiration for the award-winning movie *The French Connection*. Sonny, after his retirement, formed Grosso-Jacobson Productions and produced many successful movies and popular TV series. Years later, Sonny and I teamed up to write a screenplay for a future production.

Over the years, I got to know them all and never felt uneasy seeing, every night, the cops and mafia guys sitting there, enjoying themselves and paying little mind to one another. It was like a neutral zone, a pocket of peace in the city where they'd all come and enjoy a ceasefire and a few drinks before their endless war resumed the next day.

What a mixture it all was: cops and robbers, heroes and villains, all intertwined with an endless stream of celebrities and politicians and the average Joes, all under my watch. I don't believe there will ever be another place with such a mix. Not in my days anyway.

CHAPTER 34

The Sports Personalities

In addition to celebrities, the wise guys, and the everyday New Yorkers, the place was also a haven for sports legends, who became part of the long list of noteworthy people that I had to deal with every day. There were people like New York Jets quarterback "Broadway" Joe Willie Namath, New York Yankees owner George Steinbrenner, Mets executive and publisher Nelson Doubleday, Jr., New York Giants owner Wellington Mara, Muhammad Ali, Joe Frazier, a slew of professional wrestlers, and famous basketball players like Walt Frazier and David DeBusschere.

When the WWE, then the WWF, had wrestling nights at Madison Square Garden, the owners/promoters Vincent McMahon Sr. and his son Vincent Jr. would bring all the wrestlers to feed them late-night meals at our club. I became particularly close with the wrestler André "the Giant," who was a huge star in the early '70s. At more than seven feet tall and more than five hundred pounds, his fabled size was even more impressive in person. He wore a massive watch to fit his enormous wrist; it was like he was wearing a wall clock. No barstool or chair was big enough to hold his gargantuan body, and he preferred to stand, towering over everybody.

But for all of his physical size, his heart and his sense of humor were even bigger, and together, we used to play jokes on people we knew for laughs. For instance, I had a cousin, Nick, who always bragged about being a tough guy. He was living in New Jersey and would come to the club often with his wife, Mary. Mary was a starstruck celebrity watcher, and she preferred to sit in the cocktail lounge, amid the comings and goings of all our famous customers.

When Nick and Mary saw André for the first time, they couldn't believe their eyes, and they both looked intimidated in the presence of such a massive human being. At that moment, I thought that this was a good way for Nick to prove his toughness. So I pulled André aside and asked him to give my cousin a little scare, just as a joke. After all, I knew that André loved these opportunities as well.

He lumbered over to their table and looked down hard at Nick, who looked back up, stunned, with wide-open eyes.

"Are you making fun of me?" André said in his deep voice.

Nick just shrank back in his chair. "No, no, no, sir, not at all! I am admiring you!"

"Why? I don't look normal to you?" André demanded, still towering over Nick and staring down with a piercing gaze.

Nick got so scared that he shrank even deeper in his chair, looking over to catch my attention. I deliberately ignored him, letting him sweat a little bit until finally, I walked over to ask André if there was a problem.

"I can handle my problems," André said, without taking his eye off of Nick.

"Be careful, André, he says he's a tough guy," I said, and I started to walk away, hearing Nick protesting behind me.

"Dino, what the hell are you doing?"

"Don't expect him to help you. He started all this," André said, laughing, and then he pulled up a chair and sat with them as Nick and Mary breathed a sigh of relief. By the time the night was over, they had become friends. Afterward, Nick pulled me aside to try and convince me not to say anything to our family circle about the incident. I promised him I wouldn't as long as he never bragged again about being such a tough guy.

With André around, there were always some funny moments just waiting to happen. His humor was spontaneous and entertaining. For example, he had a pretty little blonde girlfriend, who must have been a quarter of his size, and whenever he was ready to leave, he would pick her up, place her under his arm, and walk out with her like a child clinging to a rag doll.

André was never afraid to use his size to make us all laugh, and I'll never forget the time that he once helped me, jokingly, enforce the rules of the club. It was during the hot summer months, when we relaxed the dress code a little, allowing people to enter without a tie. But there was one rule that never changed: to enter, men needed a dress jacket, and there were no exceptions. In the coatroom, we had a selection of dress jackets ready, and the coatroom girl would offer them up to those who forgot or who didn't know the rule so that they could still get in.

One night, a couple came in, but the guy wasn't wearing a jacket, and when the coatroom girl told him to pick one from the selection, he refused. I was by my desk talking to André, and the guy came up to me, complaining that he had made a reservation and was not told about the dress code. Honestly, I understood the guy's problem, but I had to stand by our rule.

"Sir, you are talking to the wrong person. This is the person you should complain to," I said, pointing up to André, who was standing next to us, towering.

But before the guy even had a chance to make his case, André jumped in. "If I'm wearing a jacket, everyone else should too," he told him in a thunderous voice.

The guy must have had a good sense of humor or a good head on his shoulders because he decided not to pursue the issue any further. Instead, he just looked up at André, saying, "I would be a fool to argue with you, André. Let's get a jacket so I can get a table."

Always looking for a laugh, André took off his massive jacket and offered it to the guy. That broke the ice, and everybody broke into laughter. From that time on, the couple became good, steady customers. I suppose they learned that day that being able to joke around with figures like André the Giant was just one of the many perks of life at Jimmy Weston's, and that putting on a jacket was just a small entry fee.

There was a constant stream of sports stars and personalities who walked by my desk in those days, and André wasn't the only one who I'd become friendly with. It's funny, sometimes, for me to think of that day when I was serving in the Army, still adjusting to American life and learning for the first time what a baseball field was. I'd ultimately become more intimately familiar with America's sports world than I ever would have imagined. I became engrossed in sports, largely because of those long nights, laughing with friends whose heads were glued to the screen, as the final moments of a big game played out. But it was also because I got to know the very people who kept that sports world turning. And those friendships meant more to me than any game ever could.

For instance, I had become familiar with sportscaster Howard Cosell even before he began spending his time there with Roone Arledge, Don Meredith, and Frank Gifford to plot the legendary birth of Monday Night Football. Cosell spent many long evenings at the place and liked to heckle me, just like he did in his interviews with sports legends.

I liked Cosell for his impressive vocabulary and his fast-talking nature, especially when he used words that I found difficult to understand. He liked to make fun of my Greek accent, and we always zinged each other and bickered over little things for fun in a way that I'm sure both of us enjoyed. It was like we were always getting into verbal sparring matches with each other, and we always looked forward to the next duel.

Cosell always wanted to sit at Table 18, but he never made a reservation. And every time, he would act cranky and come over to scold me.

"You gave my table away again?" he'd complain after seeing that Table 18 was taken.

"Howard," I would tell him, "there's a new invention out now that you should know about. It's called a telephone. Call me, and I'll put your name down and we'll hold the table for you. And don't worry about the cost of the call. I'll give you the dime back."

"All right, wise guy, I'd do that if you could spell my name correctly," Howard would say back before heading back to the bar to catch up with his martinis. Soon, he'd forget all about his favorite table and eventually sit anywhere. After all the fuss, I don't think Cosell sat at Table 18 more than twice in all the years he came there.

Of all the sports legends, none were bigger than George Steinbrenner. I can still remember the first time I met him. He and I would go on to have a long friendship together, and he was one of many stars whose paths fortuitously crossed with mine, yielding unexpected and positive results. But the first day that I met him, he had just bought the Yankees. It was 1973 when Jimmy came in with George strolling behind him.

"Dino, this is George Steinbrenner. He owns the Yankees," Jimmy told me.

I remember George looking at Jimmy with an expression like *What?* "Is that what I'm known for?" he asked.

Steinbrenner was close friends with Jimmy, and he came in frequently. He was friendly and genial at the club, didn't drink and never stayed too late. The legends about him being hyper focused on winning were true. No matter how the game turned out the night before, he was stoic and serious when he talked about baseball, like a father withholding approval.

"They better produce," he would say. "They better earn their pinstripes."

That was especially true when they played the Boston Red Sox. Those were "must-win" games, George would say.

He was very proud of the Yankees, and loved to win, but perhaps even more so, he hated to lose. In the later years, when the Yankees were unstoppable, losses were uncommon. But he would be frustrated all the same.

"Hey, George, don't worry. They're going to win the series," I would tell him.

"I know that, but they still shouldn't have lost," George would snap back.

He loved to join Jimmy and his cronies at the bar, which was Jimmy's all-time favorite place. There, Jimmy would be surrounded with friends eager to hear or tell hilarious stories, like the one about Boots, or others about Sinatra, or about the time when I left the place open at four in the morning to escort Sinatra to the Waldorf and returned to find two juiced up couples waiting at the bar.

For George, the place was like a mini Yankee Stadium, where he could be the Yankees owner but could also relax with friends and Yankees fans. He gave us big publicity once by holding a press conference there to announce the signing of famous slugger Dave Winfield, and he came back frequently to celebrate many World Series championships.

While George was one of my closest friends from the sports world, there were so many others who would brighten my nights. One of them was the ever-famous Yankee, "Mr. October" himself, Reggie Jackson.

Reggie was a big Yankees star who had become a household name by being at the center of historic Yankees moments, like when he hit three homeruns in a World Series game. He even had a candy bar named after him, called the "Reggie Bar." He fell in love with the place from the first time he came in, and I treated him like a star, placing him at Table 17 when Frank wasn't in town. Eventually, we got to know each other well, and Reggie made himself at home, developing a gag where he would stand near my desk so that whenever the phone rang, he would pick it up and begin playing maître d'.

"Good evening, Jimmy Weston's. Reggie Jackson speaking," he'd say, shocking the callers, and proceeding to take their reservations. Many times, the callers would question him, and I could hear Reggie confirming.

"Yes, yes it's me, Reggie Jackson. I'll see you when you come in."

Some of them said they thought it was a joke until they came in and saw Reggie standing there, taking phone calls. They would start chattering between themselves: *It really was him!*

Then, they would be excited to meet and talk with Reggie.

Jimmy and I loved it. It was great for business.

This went on for some time, becoming a regular joke whenever Reggie came in, so one day, I decided to have some fun with him. There were some public telephones on the wall, not too far from the desk. When Reggie wasn't looking, I dialed the number of the club, and I watched Reggie pick up the phone.

"Good evening. Jimmy Weston's. Reggie Jackson speaking."

"Who?" I said, disguising my voice.

"Reggie Jackson," he answered, sounding a little disappointed. "Can I help you?"

"Yes, I want to make a reservation."

"Sure. How many in your party?"

"One. And I want Table 17."

Reggie knew that Table 17 was not to be doled out to anybody. I could tell as I watched him that he was legitimately hesitant about how to respond.

"You can't have Table 17 unless you are Frank Sinatra, or me," he said, grinning.

"Since when did Jimmy Weston's start letting overrated ballplayers sit at Table 17?" I asked him.

Of course, as I expected, Reggie didn't take this very well. "Where have you been, buddy? In some third-world country watching some other Reggie Jackson?" he asked, getting enraged.

"Reggie, turn around and say hello to your fan," I said in my regular voice.

He turned around, and when we made eye contact, Reggie looked like he wanted to playfully throw the phone at me. After that, before answering the phone, he would look over to the public phones to see if it was me calling.

Before I met George, Reggie, and other famous Yankees like Billy Martin, my only experience with baseball had been the game I had seen in Fort Knox, and so baseball was still kind of foreign to me. But being around them quickly changed that; I'd get caught up in the cool October air, the expectation of the Fall Classic, the dog pile of players out by the pitcher's mound, celebrating the World Series, of which the Yankees won many. The baseball field in Fort Knox had once seemed so foreign to me; now, Yankee Stadium became a cathedral of sorts for me, carrying magic and electrified by the personality of my friend George.

And there were the nights when George Steinbrenner would walk in to a standing ovation, proud as a peacock to celebrate yet another Yankee World Series win, as Tommy would lead the crowd in singing, "For He's a Jolly Good Fellow" and the celebration would go on into the morning.

The truth was, I loved being around those sports personalities, hearing their stories and seeing what kind of people they were when they weren't competing in their sport. I always remember seeing Muhammad Ali, for instance, reciting poems about his upcoming fights, sending the crowd into hysterics. Ali was as great an entertainer as he was a fighter. He brought on some unforgettable moments. One time, out of curiosity, I asked him how many days a week he spends in training.

Ali then hit me with one of his most popular lines:

"Don't count the days. Make the days count."

CHAPTER 35

Tragedy

Running Jimmy Weston's wasn't always smooth sailing. For all the good times and the love that filled the place, we had our occasional patches of stormy seas, and being the maître d' presented a fair amount of challenges. Every night, I had to manage the diverse needs of very powerful people from all walks of life. Yes, there were the movie stars, the athletes, and the everyday New Yorkers who've filled me with wonderful memories of glitz, glam, and drama. But there were also the bosses of the mafia, the divas, and those wannabes who wanted special treatment, and whose demands could make the job a little difficult. And it was my job to keep up a delicate balancing act to make sure our ship stayed afloat.

Even now as I recount those occasional situations, I could never complain. Instead, handling everything was exactly why I was there, and I was good at it.

There were the times when the always-colorful Yankee manager Billy Martin, Jimmy, me, and Toots Shor would drink until the wee hours of the morning, and everyone in the place would plan to bet against the Yankees the next day as they watched Billy staying out late, putting his drinks away like a Gatorade.

"Hey, Dino," Billy said to me as he was leaving, "don't listen to those losers. We are going to win today."

And he went straight to the stadium afterward to manage the Yankees to another win.

There was the time when, the ever-popular comedian, Bob Hope, toasted a guy we called "Punchy Harry," the club's limo driver and an ex pug, thanking him for beating him senseless in the ring and forcing him to switch to comedy.

There were nights when the wise guys would come, unannounced, and demand certain tables. I would bend a little and do the best I could, but I'd never give them tables that were already reserved.

"Sit here," I'd tell them. "And when better tables become available, I'll move you there."

I'd always keep my promise and we got along fine.

And there was the night when Muhammad Ali walked in with Joe Frazier right after their "Thriller in Manila" fight, which Ali won. These two warriors fought three brutal fights, and in the ring, they wanted to kill each other. But I could see the respect and the admiration they shared for each outside the ring.

"I like Joe," Ali said. "He brings out the best of me."

"Your best will not be enough the next time," Joe joked with his thousand-watt smile.

It was indeed a glamorous job I had, rubbing elbows with all the famous and the infamous, from the Rat Pack to the heavy weight champions of the world. Every night, I looked forward to coming to work, but it wasn't just because of my unfettered access to this exclusive atmosphere. It was also because those famous personalities became some of my closest friends, and they created a truly unique and extraordinary environment, where I truly felt accepted and respected, and where I got to experience the amazing melting pot of American life in a way that few ever could.

Of course, I was also making plenty of money. I bought a nice home for us in Queens. I was supporting my family and all the while still sending money home to my relatives in Greece. It had been years since I'd seen my familial home, the rolling mountainside of Valtesiniko, and the house above my father's old store, but I never forgot my core mission in coming to America.

At the same time, Agnes was keeping a jubilant loving home that became the core of my life. Together, we worked hard to ensure that our daughters grew up in a blissful carefree childhood.

The friendships that I forged at Jimmy Weston's were special. But it was nothing compared to the family that I came home to every day: my best friends and companions, Agnes, Effie, and Olga. Coming home to them just reaffirmed to me the gifts that my new country had brought. We had a warm, loving home, our daughters were going to school, becoming educated, and most importantly, happy. I could feel the warm feeling of a bright future full of happiness all over me. We were living the ideal American Dream; it was a dream that had gone far beyond anything I could have ever imagined.

But amid the rise of fortune and prestige, tragedy struck again. Agnes was only forty-one years old and full of life when she suddenly started to not feel well, complaining of an unbearable pain that would not go away. After many tests, she was diagnosed with cancer, and we placed her in the best hospital we knew for immediate surgery.

At that time, cancer was known to be a sure killer, and all the treatments were still experimental. So when we heard that word, "cancer," it felt like there had been an earthquake, permanently shifting our idyllic world and causing our dreams to tumble to the ground.

Still, with my daughters Effie, fifteen, and Olga, eleven, we kept vigil, praying and hoping that Agnes would be okay, and that we would soon return home so we could continue the happy life that we had all started together. The three of us would visit and spend days waiting next to Agnes, hoping the doctors would finally allow us to take her home again.

But Agnes's condition deteriorated, and her pain only got worse. With the doctor's recommendation, Effie's and Olga's visits had to stop, and soon, all I could do was sit day and night by Agnes's bedside, trying to comfort her.

One early Sunday morning, I was called out of the room to meet a team of doctors from Memorial Sloan Kettering Center Hospital who had come unexpectedly. When I met them, the lead doctor and administrator, Dr. Beattie, told me that they had been sent by a "friend" to help, but he would not say who it was. I didn't really press him to tell me because at this desperate juncture, there was no time for questions, and I would welcome any help offered. However, I had a feeling in my gut who the "friend" was.

Dr. Beattie and his team wasted no time. They examined Agnes and immediately made recommendations to Dr. Sorensen, Agnes's attending doctor. But for reasons that could only be attributed to his personal ego, he ignored Dr. Beattie's recommendations. I suppose he felt that he'd been shown up by this team of higher-tier doctors who had come to his hospital, and he apparently valued his pride over the health of his patient, and for three days after that, Dr. Sorensen didn't even visit Agnes as her suffering continued.

I became furious and went into a rage. Maybe I lost it for a while because my anger for this guy made me ignore all consequences, and I set out like a possessed man, trying to find him and tear his heart out. Lucky for him, he was nowhere to be found, and security eventually came over to question me. Then I realized that Agnes's survival was the most important thing at that time, and I was cursing myself for wasting such valuable time looking for a worthless bum.

I contacted Dr. Beattie, who immediately made arrangements for an ambulance to transfer Agnes to Memorial Sloan Kettering. It was there that my gut feelings were confirmed about the secret friend because as I walked into the lobby, I read an inscription on a large marble plaque that read: "All services in this institution made possible by the Frank Sinatra Foundation."

Under Dr. Beattie's care, Agnes began to regain composure, and she became strong enough to have another operation that made her comfortable enough to be able to see her daughters again, and that made her so happy. But Dr. Beattie's diagnosis was not encouraging, and I am sure now that Agnes realized that her end was very near. But she loved us so much and never showed any fear. Instead, she tried to give us courage and hope, always with a loving smile.

"Educate the girls," she whispered to me before she took her last breath.

"I promise you," I told her, but I don't think she heard me.

I will never forget those moments; they were the most sacramental moments of my life, and they guided me to keep my promise.

At first, Agnes's death felt like a bad dream. But when reality started to sink in, it was devastating for all three of us. Although my promise to Agnes kept me going, I felt like I was suffocating, like someone had taken my very ability to breathe. I felt a dark and familiar feeling bubbling up from inside, those same feelings of rage and anger that I'd felt as a child, only now, there was no clear enemy. There was no Stasinopoulos with his scraggly beard or Kokkinis with his death list. As a child, I was able to focus the pain of my father's death on my longing for revenge, and I set out to find justice. Back then, I thought that nothing could be worse than failing to get my revenge. But now, I had found out that there was something worse: losing Agnes to cancer, an evil that has no face and that could never be brought to justice. It was frustrating.

One day, an unexpected call came from Dorothy Uhlemann, who told me that "Mr. S." was in town and wanted to invite us for a visit to his residence at the Waldorf Towers. I had never been to Frank's place before, and when we reached the twenty-second floor, Frank was standing by the door, waiting for us with warm hugs and kisses. Somehow, with his unique way, he made us completely forget that we were about to enter the private residence of one of the most popular megastars of the century. Instead, it felt like we were entering the warm home of a good friend.

This was all totally unexpected, but we spent hours together like one big family. Frank recalled many of his own life's ups and downs, especially the sudden death of his mother and how he coped with it. It was all moving, timely and uplifting, and from that moment on, we would owe a debt of gratitude to the Chairman. It would not be the last time that we owed him more gratitude than we could repay.

Afterward, every time I saw our "friend," I tried to bring up his kindness, to thank him for his loyal support and the way that he had helped make our lives easier in those difficult times. But he always cut me off. Sinatra had a unique code of words, a code that only his close friends understood. I can still hear his words every time I think of those times.

"Lights out, Greek," he'd tell me.

That meant that the conversation must come to an end, and it always did.

That was the kind of guy Sinatra was. He was fiercely loyal, and his friends and family came before all else. But he was quiet about it. To him, loyalty and kindness weren't some badges of honor to be boasted about at bars. They were acts of friendship that he held close to his heart and rarely disclosed. And whether it was that evening getting pizza for the homeless in Harlem or his actions in helping my family, Frank felt no need to brag or accept thanks for his good deeds. In a friendship with Frank Sinatra, loyalty and kindness came for free, and there was no need to discuss it.

CHAPTER 36

Strangers in My Homeland

For us, as time went on, things weren't getting any better. We all missed Agnes and tried to comfort each other, but still, she would never be forgotten. In fact, I put an inscription on her tombstone that described exactly how we all felt:

"We love you and we will miss you more than yesterday—less than tomorrow."

After so many years, this promise remains though there are times that I wished I had never had it written. Some promises are better left unspoken.

A few years before Agnes's death, we had taken a short trip to Greece. It was the first time I had been back there since I left after the war, and it was a trip filled with happiness and a warm reunion with family. It was especially exciting for Effie and Olga, who were meeting and playing with their cousins for the first time.

Now, remembering that happy trip, I thought it would be a good idea to take the girls and visit Greece again so that we could spend some time with the tight-knit family that I had never forgotten since childhood. I felt that we needed a change and that a longer trip could provide us with a much-needed respite that could help us restore the balance of our lives. When I mentioned the trip to Effie and Olga, I could see that they were excited to see their cousins again. I knew then it was the right thing to do, and we planned to stay there for the whole summer.

By this time, my siblings had all moved to Athens, where we were welcome to stay with them. But my heart was in Valtesiniko, which I had remembered as the most beautiful little village that I had ever seen in spite of all the tragedy that had happened there. I wanted to stay in my parents' house, climb up that old concrete staircase my father built and walked along every day to go back and forth to his store, to sleep on that old wooden bed, to get up in the morning and splash my face with that cool clean water and breathe that crisp mountain air, to feel like I was home again. I wanted a whole summer away from New York's and Athens's busy streets and tall buildings so I could see my daughters playing with their little cousins, chasing sheep and riding donkeys in the countryside. I wanted to fill my heart with that wonderful feeling of childhood, the childhood that I'd lost that faithful day in May 1944. All the while, my siblings were reluctant to travel together out to Valtesiniko, and I couldn't quite understand why. I planned to take a bus from Athens on my own until my brother, Pavlo, finally offered to take us all there with the truck he was using for his furniture business, which he ran with my sister Kaiti.

I remember that the truck ride was bumpy and dusty, but we had fun, piling up on one another every time the truck hit a bump or took a sharp turn as it traveled through the rugged mountains. I couldn't contain my excitement, and with every thump, that image of our house in the mountains grew more vivid. Soon I'd be home, and so I didn't mind the bumpy ride.

Finally, the truck made its final stop in front of the house, and I was the first to get off, anxious and ready to see the home that I still thought about all the time, even from my home across the sea. But on my first look, I froze in my tracks. I could feel disappointment bubbling up inside me. The house in front of me was far different from the home I had been longing to see. It was so different that my first thought was that we had arrived at the wrong place. The store on the ground floor that my father loved so much was now gone, and the cement staircase he climbed every night to come upstairs at the end of the day was gone. The whole front of the house was defaced and destroyed, and a new house was attached to its side.

Hurt and disappointed, I held my tongue. I couldn't even find the energy to ask what had happened. I just walked inside quickly, hoping to at least see if the interior was still anything like the home as I knew it. But that wasn't the case. The warm family house I remembered, where all of us were born and raised, shared good times and survived bad times, was no longer the house I remembered. My father's store and the middle floor were converted to living spaces, and it felt like a house full of strangers.

Without a word, I went to get some sleep that night, hoping that the next day would bring something different. As I was drifting to sleep, I thought of the large vineyard that my father owned on a hillside just outside of the village. It was his pride and joy, and I remembered how he would hire many of the villagers to harvest its grapes and produce huge barrels of wine.

In the morning, after I learned that my brother had already left for business, I took a stroll to visit the vineyard, hoping that seeing the old patch of land would bring me some comfort. But when I got there, I found it totally destroyed. A once thriving, beautiful, green, and rich field of memories now turned into ruins of dead branches and dirt.

I stood there, searching for answers, but around me I could find no clues to tell me what had happened. Then I saw an old man coming up the road, and I asked him if he knew why the vineyard was destroyed.

"Son," he said with bitterness in his voice, "I fed my family for many years by working here, but its owners took big money from European Union to uproot it."

I learned later that this was a program that the European Community had offered Greek farmers across the country. All over, farmers took similar deals, all of which helped lead to the disastrous state of Greece's economy.

I watched the old man walk away while shaking his head, and as I stayed behind, staring at the tattered remains of the vineyard, all those terrible events of May 1 flashed before my eyes. I thought about what my father would think seeing this. And now I felt guilty that I had ever left, that I had ever let this happen. I felt compelled to go to his grave, to apologize for leaving it all behind and going to America. America was a dream he'd always wanted for me. But it seemed to have come at great cost.

Later that day, I spoke to more villagers and learned that the vineyard wasn't the only plot of land that we had lost. Other farming plots owned by my father were sold and traded away. I would have understood the reasons if there were a severe need. But it frustrated me that me and my two sisters, who were also living in America, were kept in the dark. And even now as adults, we continued to be kept in the dark.

I tried to get some answers from my sister Kaiti, but she always gave me the same response: "What is done is already done. Don't bother asking about it."

My questions were purely sentimental, but by asking them, I had given the impression that I had come back to Greece to claim my share of inheritance, and over the course of my trip, they began to treat me like I was an outsider, the American who had everything and who had no need to be a part of our family's inheritance. I had been gone too long, and all the money I had sent back did not erase what the communists had done. I had become a stranger in my homeland.

It was a painful experience; even more heart-wrenching was when I heard my sister sympathizing with the families of the communists who killed our father. "They should not have been opposed," she said one day. "They were patriots also. They were fighting the Germans." She just ignored the fact that the Germans left Greece on their own while the communist rebels were killing more innocent Greeks than the Germans did. I felt everything, from our house to our history, being erased.

I decided that I should leave, and I returned to America as a disheartened man. I hadn't lived in Greece for so long, but it had always been such a big part of my identity. The story of my life there, the hardship that I faced, and the family that I left behind underpinned all of the success that I'd had in America. And now I felt that it had been pulled away from me, and that was painful. But I had two little daughters to take care of all by myself, so I began the painstaking process of putting my life together again. So I went back to my old job at Jimmy Weston's and reconnected with my old friends.

I was glad to see that nothing had changed, and I found myself sitting again with people at the bar deep into the night, or over at Table 17 with Frank, Jilly, and Jimmy. Other nights were spent talking baseball with Steinbrenner or talking with Anthony Quinn about possibly making a sequel to his movie *Zorba the Greek*. In these especially hard times, when my old home felt foreign to me, it was like I had found a new family.

However, somehow the trip to Greece had changed me, and as hard as I tried, it was a struggle for me to blend in again. Many deep wells of emotion were reopened. The death of Agnes, the memories of betrayals in my hometown, the murder of my father, and all the demons of my past returned in vivid color to haunt me. Lost and bereft of my spiritual and emotional compass, I turned to the bottle to drown out those unwelcome memories and to erase the knowledge that my loving wife was dead.

Alcohol worked for me. It made my brain cloudy. I could still feel all of the demons surrounding me, but it felt like I was watching them from inside an unbreakable glass cage, like I was observing them from a safe distance, acknowledging their presence while knowing that they wouldn't bother me as long as the scotch I was drinking was there to protect me. In scotch, I had found a new friend that I always could depend on, who never refused me when I called, especially at the club, where its presence was always just a few feet away. Little did I know that alcohol would eventually take me to a very low and depressed place.

Drinking made me feel good, but not happy. I'd look around our club at all the happy drinkers and wondered why I could never feel as happy as they did. I tried to get drunk and embrace the feeling of it, to become carefree like the others who came through our place, but it never worked. The more I drank, the more depressed, unsociable, and angry I became, and frankly, I found myself liking it. Years later, I found out that that's what booze does to you when you rely on it to solve your problems.

It was late one night; I was sitting and drinking with the dangerous Dennis and his crew. Dennis and I, at this point, had become much more comfortable around each other, and that initial guardedness of our first meeting had subsided into a casual familiarity. And while I knew that it wasn't a good idea to be seen close to someone like Dennis, at this time in my life, I would sit and drink with anybody.

I suppose Dennis had seen what I was going through, and he could tell by my drinking habits that there were clearly some deep-rooted problems that I was trying to undo, and so he offered me a new remedy:

"You should try some coke," he said.

What the hell, I thought. *Why not?*

In fact, I knew a few people like Dennis who were regular cocaine users, and they all seemed to go through life as if it was all just wine and roses. And so, I thought, maybe, this could become a new remedy for me, something stronger and happier than alcohol. I followed Dennis to the men's room, and to my surprise, Boots immediately seemed to know why we had come in there, and he stayed by the door to alert us if someone was entering.

Dennis took out a vial of cocaine, took two deep sniffs, and then handed it to me.

"Here, try it, you'll like it," he said.

As soon as I took that sniff, it was like a whole new world opened in front of me. Everything around me became clear, and I felt like I was a different person. It wasn't like the alcohol. It was instantaneous, and it felt like I had burst from that glass cage and chased all those demons away. I was free. And from that night on, cocaine and scotch became my way to carefree living.

Each night, cocaine took more power over me, and I never realized that it started a downward spiral that was leading toward a total destruction. I didn't notice that I was neglecting my job, my cares and parenting, as well as my accountability to my friends. I was spending more and more of my money on buying cocaine from Dennis, without ever thinking twice about how much I had thrown away.

There were times when I would panic because my supply was at its end and Dennis and his guys weren't around to get more. So I'd run to a phone and desperately call them. If I didn't get more, I would become muddy, feel sick to my stomach, start sweating, and lose control of my speech until I got my next hit. And each time, that white powder tightened its noose on my life.

I was hooked, and I didn't even know it.

CHAPTER 37

Strung Out

I became so strung out; I couldn't recognize that I was on the verge of destroying everything that I was living for: my daughters, my well-being, and my self-respect. I thought that I had found some kind of relief in the drugs and the drinking, but it was actually just masking a deep-seated rage. I was consumed with anger and lashing out at everyone for no real reason, all the while convincing myself that everything was fine.

There was one evening for instance when I beat up a meter maid outside the club for ticketing my car ten minutes before the legal time to park was up. I didn't realize the guy was just doing his job. I didn't care about that, and I certainly didn't think of the consequences. I just attacked him and beat him up badly. It could have been worse, but thanks to Jimmy and his many connections, the case was settled.

These kinds of blow-ups were becoming increasingly common for me, and I was always on the edge of a bout of rage. I remember feeling that, unless it was cocaine or a drink, it was just a waste of time, a distraction from the fake happiness that I was consuming every day. I thought everything was great, and I had no idea that I had stopped caring about my daughters. I thought they were too young to understand what I was doing, too young to suspect that I was capable of living such a reckless life, but I was fooling myself. They could see all the changes in me and didn't know what to do.

I didn't realize it, but many of my friends started to turn away from me, and others were watching me from a distance. I couldn't grasp the fact that me, the guy who knew everybody and who every-body wanted to know, had now become a very angry man who only saw others through a hazy cloud of selfishness. And the only comfort for me was a vial of coke, plenty of scotch, and a gun that Dennis gave me to carry. Carrying a gun felt good to me, and it reminded me of those days as a ten-year-old, clinging to that machine gun in the wall of my father's store, as if it represented some sort of liberation or some sort of justice.

I knew that Dennis was a pretty smart fellow for the business he was in, and he knew that as long as I had that gun with me, while he was at the club, he always had access to one in case he needed it. And with me being so strung out, I didn't even realize that I'd become a gun mule for Dennis. He connected me with a guy I got to know as Mike Moose from whom I'd get my supply of coke. The transactions always occurred in the men's room, using Boots as a lookout who was also turned onto coke.

I had now become aware of the drug racket occurring right in our club. But rather than stop it, I embraced it and took part in it. It was very convenient for me, having Mike Moose bringing over the stuff to me and having Boots as a partner in crime. But sometimes, if I ran out of supply before I could meet with Moose, I would get irritable, moody, and ready to pounce until I got my hit. Many times, I'd seek out Dennis and get a hit from him.

There was a time when I was a man at his peak who ran a tight, clean ship, uncorrupted by drugs; I never would have allowed this to happen. But I didn't care anymore. I'm sure that Jimmy, as a former undercover narcotics cop, knew what was going on. But he also knew well of Dennis and the Westies' reputation, so he just looked away.

Thinking back on all that now, I can say that the only thing that stood between me and a destructive abyss was my daughters' uncon-ditional love and the loyalty of one friend who refused to let me go. Lost in a haze of vice and pain, I didn't see that there was one person who was noticing how I was changing. He kept watching me, and while others started to steer clear from me, he started coming back to the place more often, observing me from a distance.

It was Frank Sinatra, and in his typical way, he came to me one night as a loyal friend who would never walk away, and in doing so, he helped save my life. As usual, he was at Table 17 with Jilly, keeping an eye on me. There was a time when the sound of their laughter and the sight of their smiling faces would entice me to go over and sit with them for a bit for a quick chat. But on this night, I had run out of coke and was pacing around nervously, slowly starting to panic.

To my relief, Dennis and his crew walked in, and I rushed to escort them, as always, to Table 23, which was directly across and in full view of Table 17. I knew that soon, Dennis would be going to the men's room and I could get a hit from him. I knew that if I could just get a hit again, I'd feel better, and then I could be sociable and join my friends at Table 17.

As soon as I saw Dennis get up to go to the men's room, I rushed right in behind him and followed him into the restroom, and while Boots stood by the door, Dennis handed me a vial. Quickly, with trembling hands, I got ready to take a sniff, but then I noticed that someone else had entered the men's room and was now standing right next to me. I was stunned to see it was Frank Sinatra, staring hard at me with an angry and disappointed look on his face.

I was caught red-handed, and there was no denial.

He ordered Dennis to get out and told Boots to stay outside and not let anyone in.

As astonished as I was, I became dismayed when Dennis obeyed Sinatra's orders and left quietly. Then I realized that Frank Sinatra was the only person I knew who could order Dennis around without any fear.

"You are a man and a father, so start acting like one," Sinatra snapped at me with anger in his voice.

Then he grabbed the vial out of my hand and tossed it on the counter. I just stood there, searching for the right words to say, but I couldn't find any.

"This is your choice, pal. It's now or never. I don't walk with losers," he demanded.

It was the word *"loser"* that hit me like a lightning bolt. In that moment, I felt like I could see myself for the first time and truly understood how pitiful I'd become. I'd also realized that I was about to lose the best friend I ever had, and that thought shook me to the core. I thought of our long nights sitting at Table 17, our trip to Harlem, his generous effort to help save Agnes, his invitation to his home, his crooning voice greeting me at the desk: "Hey, Greek." And yet just a few minutes earlier, I'd ignored him like he was nobody just so I could get my hit.

For the first time since Agnes died, the anger stopped, just for a moment, and I had a brief instance of clarity. I knew that I couldn't allow myself to continue with coke and booze and be a good father to my daughters. I couldn't keep my promise to Agnes, be a good friend, or have self-respect. In that moment, seeing in front of me the true loyalty of a true friend, I made a choice.

I picked up the vial from the counter and emptied it into the sink. It was something that I would have never imagined I could ever do. There was that anger inside me that was always raging. It raged when my father died, and it took years to break free. And now, after my wife died, it'd been raging again, and I thought it would never stop.

As I poured the coke into the drain, I could feel that anger one last time, in one brief moment, wanting desperately to scoop it up again. But as I watched the coke dissolve down the drain, I felt something unexpected. I felt lighter and happier. For the first time in a long time, I knew I made the right choice, and it had set me free.

I became encouraged when Sinatra spoke again.

"I'll trust you, but don't cross me," he said.

His words were strong, firm, and they were clearly understood.

"I promise," I told him, hoping he'd believe me and understanding that our friendship would survive as long as I kept my promises. No other words were spoken; we embraced each other with silent promises that we both knew were true.

After that, Sinatra left the men's room, calm and cool, but all fired up inside.

"Keep a clean house, Boots," I heard him tell Boots before he went back to Table 17. I could tell by looking at Boots's face that he understood also.

But Frank never left anything unfinished. He ignored Dennis's lethal reputation and called him to Table 17 for a very short conversation. I never knew what was said. All I could see was a very serious Sinatra and an unusually suppressed Dennis. Whatever it was, the talk was very short and effective. Soon, Dennis returned to his table, and he and his gang strolled out of the club. I never saw them again.

Sinatra's intervention lasted only thirty minutes, but it'd leave the impact of a lifetime on me. I kept my promise, and I never looked back. For those who've struggled with drug abuse, it's often a common story; it's a sickness that takes you through many rehab treatments and painful times, and most of those who experienced it would probably never believe that I had come out of it so instantly, so permanently. But it's true.

My rehab treatments were always in front of me. My daughters, for a long time, helplessly watched my health and my fortitude spiral downward without knowing why or how. They were now traumatized and feared that after losing their mother, they'd lose their father too and be left all alone in the world. Now I could see them feeling secure, happy again. We became closer than ever, and they became my best motivation for recovery.

The word "loser" never left my thoughts, and I got to know that the most powerful weapon in the world is the human brain, if you put it to work for you. Of course, there were times when I felt that anger, and that urge for a hit and a drink, when that angry man inside me started to rage for attention. But my brain was there to remind me who was in charge. I never took it for granted again, and there was never a need for treatments and rehabs.

One icy, cold, and snowy, late Sunday night, I was home when I realized I had run out of cigarettes. It made me feel anxious, like an itch I couldn't quite scratch, so despite the weather, I got in my car to go to a store and buy a pack. It was not an easy task. The streets were so slippery and icy, and I had some close calls getting to the store.

I lit my first cigarette and started going back home, but this time I wouldn't be so lucky. My car slid and hit another car. Now, I was getting shucked with snow, standing out in the freezing cold to exchange information with the other driver, and when I finally got home, I reached for another cigarette, but before I lit it, my brain reminded me that it was that cigarette that had caused a night's worth of bad experiences. Instead of lighting the cigarette, I started talking to it.

"You," I started saying. "You made me leave my warm house and go out in this bad weather, got me into an accident, only to find you and bring you here. You may think you have control over me. But let me tell you something. Nobody controls Dino."

I crushed the cigarette; I smashed the whole pack, and I threw it all into the garbage. It was again that mighty brain that reminded me that I was in control, and instantly I felt the glory of being free. Surely, there were times when I felt those powerful urges for cigarettes, but the brain again stepped in, and I never touched cigarettes again.

Promises were kept and life went on.

CHAPTER 38

The Lean Years

After a glorious nineteen-year run at Jimmy Weston's, things started to change slowly. Many of our long-time customers were getting older and started to come less often as others passed away, and the warm and lively nights became more infrequent. Meanwhile, all around us, disco places were sprouting up, attracting a younger crowd that much preferred to patronize in such loose places, where they could walk in with jeans and sneakers, listen to loud disco music, and enjoy drinking their beer out of the bottle. And as they started to flock toward this new trend, the old guard of the classy supper clubs like ours became the target of extinction.

It was a bittersweet time, and I remember well those quiet moments, looking out over a room of empty tables that were once the hottest tickets in town, watching desolate dance floor where thousands of happy couples once twirled and trotted, and spotting a scattered few souls sitting at the cocktail lounge, once full with gamblers and sports enthusiasts alike, keeping our bartenders always busy especially during the Monday Night Football game. Now, all I could see was our bartender Joe with hardly anything to do.

Those days, I had plenty of time and often found myself sitting at Table 17, reminiscing about the past, as the memories of familiar faces would seemingly glide before me like unsettled ghosts. One late night, I glanced over to the bar and saw four lonely people sitting there, like they had nowhere else to go, and for some reason, it brought me back to a night in 1983 when Frank came in with four other people, and he was drinking and smoking heavily, having just recently been crushed by the news that his good friend and musical director Don Costa had died. It was around closing time, and he wanted to be alone, so he ordered his limo driver to take everyone in his company home and then return. He sat alone at Table 17, pouring himself stiff drinks out of the bottle, drinking with no sign of ever stopping.

The place had emptied out; all our workers had gone home, and Frank asked me for another bottle of Jack Daniels, but as I looked at him, disheveled and depressed, I realized that it was now my turn to intervene. I knew that there was no one person who could tell Sinatra what to do, and I knew Frank could get furious, but I didn't care. He stood up for me once, and now I had to stand up for him, regardless of how difficult it might have been.

Instead of bringing him the bottle, I told him that he should stop drinking, eat something, and go get some sleep. To my surprise, he didn't react at all. There was no explosion of anger, not even an argument or a protest. Maybe he realized that once he had done the same for me and I had listened to him, but I'll never know; we never talked about it. He just looked at me with teary eyes and asked me for a pen. I gave him my pen, and without saying anything, he slowly started to write on the tablecloth.

"Don Costa, he was a good man," he wrote.

Then it was like a dam had broken. He started to cry like a baby, like it was something he'd wanted to do for a long time, as if he was spending every tear that he'd held back in his life, all for this moment to memorialize the good soul of his friend Don Costa.

I stood there looking at this tough guy, Frank Sinatra, all broken up like a little kid. At first, I was surprised, but then it was clear to me that the whole scene made perfect sense. I realized then that, when it comes to friendships, Sinatra wasn't tough at all; he was all heart. And that made him vulnerable in these sensitive times. I also realized that this was exactly what he needed, why he had sent all his friends' home so he could sit there alone. He needed a good cry, on his own and away from the crowd, so that's exactly what I let him do. I just patted him on the back and let him take as much time as he wanted. I don't know how much time passed, but after a while,

Frank regained his composure; he slowly folded the tablecloth like it was an American flag, tucked it under his arm, and got up to leave. It was private, silent funeral procession; all it was missing was taps on the trumpet.

As always, I escorted him outside to his limo, but still wanted to make sure he would be okay, so I jumped in the limo with him.

"You want to kick me out, go ahead. It's your limo. I'm just riding in it," I told him jokingly.

"It'll be a long three-block ride," he said.

We arrived at his hotel at the Waldorf Towers just three blocks away, and by now I could tell he was okay. We said good night and exchanged our usual hugs, then he ordered his driver to take me back. I returned to Jimmy Weston's only to find that, in my excitement, I'd left the place open and unsupervised. It was now 5:00 a.m., and I found four lost souls were sitting at the bar, waiting for the bartender. I had a little bit of a hard time telling them that it was past the legal time to serve booze.

"Where can we go?" one asked.

"Come back tonight, and I'll buy you a drink," I told him, and they left.

I don't remember if they did come back. It was likely that they did. The place was like that, drawing lost souls like moths to a flame.

It was sad, now, watching it lose that allure and seeing it empty out, hearing the echoes off the wooden walls and tabletops as the place settled into emptiness. I would be sitting at Table 17, watching Jimmy at the bar drinking, talking and laughing, as he always did, but without the large crowd around him. I always admired him though because he kept that spark, his eagerness to joke, even as his audience started to dwindle.

Meanwhile, I'd go back and recall the good times, looking over at Table 10, where Howard Cosell and Roone Arledge once huddled regularly and came up with Monday Night Football. I could recall another time, too, where Arledge once again huddled there with Cosell and Sinatra's producer, Jerry Weintraub, to plan an unforgettable entertainment experience.

It was Sinatra's historic Main Event concert at Madison Square Garden on October 13, 1974. Frank got me four front row tickets, and I brought my wife, my eight-year-old daughter Effie, and my first cousin Patricia. The concert was a special night for millions of viewers, as well as the twenty-thousand-plus audience that packed the Garden. But it would become an enduring memory for us when at the end of the show, Frank reached out and took Effie into his arms and circled the stage with her. It was just Frank doing what he did best: giving us the memories of a lifetime.

There were lots of moments like that, which came flooding back to me every time I sat there, no matter how empty it was. Another night at Carnegie Hall, while visiting backstage, Frank had given my daughters these large silk handkerchiefs as gifts. But as we were leaving, somebody snatched Olga's handkerchief, and that set her off, and she went into a storm, running to the exit, ready to find the person. Her screams were so loud, they could be heard backstage, and so it didn't take long for security to come back and find her. But they weren't alone. Our good friend Dorothy Uhlemann came as well, and she calmed Olga down with the sweet promise that Frank would send her another. A week later, a box arrived at our house for Olga.

I could recall what ended up being the last time that we sat with Frank at Table 17. It was 1989, and he mentioned that he wanted to share his seventy-fifth birthday with his New York fans. Accustomed to doing things his way, he threw a jubilee concert on December 13, 1990 at the Byrne arena in the Meadowlands, New Jersey, near Hoboken, where he was born on December 12, 1915.

It was yet another special moment in his career that he allowed me and my family to witness. With my two daughters, we joined twenty thousand other younger fans who had come to celebrate. For me, it felt like the celebration of the end of an era, a salute to a special place across the Hudson on Fifty-Fourth Street, and all the wonderful people who filled it every night.

Suspecting that it might be the last time we would see our friend onstage, we commissioned an artist named Carol Peck to put together all of our memories in the form of a poem and gave it to him as a birthday present. Years later, I learned that Frank kept that poem with all of his awards inside his house.

I often let my thoughts take me back to those swinging years, hoping somehow that they would return and materialize in front of me in full color and form. But all I had to do was look around at that almost-empty skeleton, and I could see that the final curtain was slowly coming down.

Those swinging years flowed by so sweetly and serenely, like honey dripping from a spoon, and for a long time I thought they'd never end. But soon, faster than I could have ever imagined, it was over, and in those final days, sitting at Table 17 all by myself, I fought off feelings of sadness by resting comfortably in the oasis of memories that nineteen years had left behind. Every once in a while, I allowed myself to be proud. Immigrants who come to America searching for the American Dream. Everybody has an idea for what that dream should be. But the truth is, it's impossible to know until you get there, and everybody's dream is different. I could only hope that anybody enjoyed their dream as much as I enjoyed mine.

In those lean years, a few faithful friends and customers would occasionally come back to the place for a drink and, like me, recall those electric years of the past. But it wasn't enough to keep the place going. So in 1989, the doors of the legendary Jimmy Weston's Supper Club permanently closed. Table 17 was now just another table. And Sinatra, now older, secluded himself in his California home and never returned to New York, and Tommy Furtado and his band moved on.

Not long after the place shuttered, the man who gave it its soul followed. Jimmy Weston died a few years after closing, leaving behind a legacy. I was heartbroken, but little did I know that my next chapter was about to start.

I was very hurt at the news of Jimmy's death. It felt like losing a brother. No place in New York City was as joyful as whichever one Jimmy was at, and I sometimes feel that his death marked the end of the true supper club crowd, the guys who held the whole scene together and kept us laughing until the sun came up. I went to his memorial services feeling a bit lost when I ran into another close friend, George Steinbrenner.

At this point, Steinbrenner was in the midst of creating the unstoppable Yankee dynasty of the '90s, but I had known him much more personally. We'd become very close over our years sharing laughs at the bar, and he was one of the few who stood by me when my wife passed away, before I started to spiral out of control. Now, years later, he'd stand by me again like a brother to help me survive Jimmy's death.

I remember when we were there, and I could see that George was very sad. He wasn't talking much, probably lost in thought, sorting through his favorite memories with Jimmy, until finally, he said that something was missing from there.

"It's something that Jimmy would love to have here tonight. Do you know what that might be?" he asked me.

For more than twenty years, I had watched Jimmy thrive in the place he loved the most, and I didn't even have to think about my answer.

"He would love to have a big bar here, with all his friends around drinking," I told him.

"That's right, I'm thinking the same thing. Jimmy would have loved that," George said.

In the media, George was caricatured as a tough, hard-nosed businessman who would give you his best but always expected the best in return. And that was all true. But in his heart, he always had a soft spot for his friends. He considered Jimmy a legend and wanted Jimmy to be in a special place with other legends, so he made all the arrangements for Jimmy to be buried at Kensico Cemetery in Valhalla, New York, where the legendary Yankee Lou Gehrig is buried, along with the famous bandleader Tommy Dorsey and the funny man actor Danny Kaye, along with other notables.

After the club closed down, I was on the hunt for another job, all the while knowing that I'd never find one like the one I had at Jimmy Weston's. The disco clubs were taking over, and jobs like mine had disappeared. Then one day, I got a call from George asking me to go and see him at his office at the stadium.

I had driven to Yankee Stadium, but in all the years we knew each other, I had never been in George's office, and when I walked in,

I was immediately impressed with the many pieces of Yankee memorabilia. But the one thing that caught all my attention was a big sign on his desk. It was so visible and stood out from everything else in the office, and it was impossible to ignore. It had only a few words, but they completely captured Steinbrenner's strong personality.

"Lead, follow, or get the hell out of the way," it read with big blue letters.

I was impressed, and that day, I would find out that the meaning of that sign applied to everyone.

"I want you to run the Pinstripe Pub here at the stadium. This is up your alley, and it is something that you know and do well," George started to say, sure of himself as always, assuming that I would take the job. And without giving me a chance to say anything, he continued outlining the details of the position and already had all the necessary papers in order, along with my credentials to the stadium, which read: "Management."

It was hard to refuse. George had already made up his mind and was counting on me. It reminded me of the day that I was drafted by the US Army. Now I felt that I was being drafted by George Steinbrenner. At the end, George pointed at that sign that had caught all my attention and warned me, "Keep in mind that this goes for everybody who works here, including you."

I took one more look at that sign, and honestly, it did something to me. It motivated me, and I told myself: *No. I'm not going to be a follower. I'm going to lead.*

I spent some wonderful, happy times working for the Boss, and soon I discovered that, while working at the stadium, there was to be no socializing, no friendship, no fooling around with him. It wasn't like a night at Jimmy Weston's, it was just about doing my job and doing it well. However, when the job was done, and later we would meet by the elevator or at the parking lot, "the boss" would become the good old George again.

"Let's meet for a hamburger at P.J. Clarke's," he would say, referencing another one of his favorite places on Fifty-Fifth Street and Third Avenue. And we would unwind into the night, remembering again those glorious days at the place where we first met. But times had changed; indeed, people had died or moved on. But at our core, those of us who remembered those days, were still the same. Just give us a few drinks, a burger, and some laughs, and we'll make memories for life. Which reminds me, once again, to be thankful for being given the wisdom to make the choice to pursue *this* life.

When an opportunity arose to take another path, and like so many others, I made an initial mistake that almost cost me everything, most importantly my happiness. I entered a business venture and purchased three rides in Playland amusement park in Rye Beach, New York. I arranged with Jimmy Weston to take the summers off and found myself pouring my blood, sweat, energy, and tears into something that didn't feel quite right for me and soon realized that my heart was truly, and solely, in the club business.

And so, one morning, early before opening time at the park, I got a cup of coffee and sat at a picnic table and decided to have a talk with myself. And I listened to the misgivings in my gut. The more energy I poured into this, the more I was missing out on the opportunities for which I was destined—in Jimmy Weston's and in the entertainment business.

That day, I told my brother-in-law and business partner that I wanted out. Luckily, we were able to quickly sell the rides, and I went back to focus on where my heart was: Jimmy Weston's.

Every day I thank God I made that choice. I realized that day that I did, indeed, have a dream. And I was willing to put my whole heart into making it come true.

And I never looked back.

CHAPTER 39

End of an Era

Now, as I look back, I can say that life is like a rollercoaster that takes you through excruciating curves, through dark tunnels, down steep and sudden drops, and up to bright sunshine. There are moments that make you scream and moments that make you squeal with laughter. It's a ride that seems endless, and you wish it never ends. It's a hopeful wish, but the truth is that nothing lasts forever.

On February 6, 1997, when Jimmy Weston died, I could see myself on that rollercoaster, and I felt it starting to slow down, a signal that the ride would soon be stopping to let me off to make room for new passengers. When that time does come, I'll leave with no regrets. I had a marvelous ride and hope that all those newcomers find their rides just as thrilling.

It was at Jimmy Weston's Supper Club where most of the thrills took place, but since the beginning of 1988 and on, our club had started to change drastically, and as I started to look around at the world outside of our little oasis, I noticed that America itself had started to change too, and those wonderful American ways that I embraced the day I stepped off the *Italia* in 1952 were slowly disappearing.

I'd started to notice it among student protests, which had become more rebellious than the ones I remembered seeing back in the 1960s. I understood and supported their right to express their freedom of speech, but when I saw students marching in the streets in an uncivilized and often violent manner, protesting against the government, I found myself dismayed. This newer generation was different; they were rowdy and less patriotic, taking drastic actions such as stepping on and burning their own country's flag. Certainly, there was a time in my home country where such actions could have gotten you killed.

It was sad to see that they would never appreciate that feeling of freedom that I felt as a broken boy, when I saw those gallant Allied soldiers enter my country with the flag aloft, coming to liberate me from the tyranny of communism. And seeing that symbol of freedom stepped on and burned, it brought me to a sobering realization: it's impossible to truly appreciate freedom until freedom is lost.

And while I prayed that those young men never experience that loss, I fear they may come to take their freedom for granted.

Based on my own experience, I'd have to blame the end of the draft for the shift in America's youth. When I came to America, I was still green about life and a confused kid, when suddenly I was drafted at the age of eighteen. But two years later, I came out as a mature man, ready to endure any of the dark tunnels that my life's roller-coaster took me through. I learned discipline, self-respect, respect for others, but most importantly, I learned perseverance. Those key facets became the pivot points of my life, lessons that I could have never learned in any college. The military was the hammer that forged maturity out of a young man from the mold of a disorganized child, and I owe all of my successes to those two years of military service.

As my rollercoaster keeps slowing down, it leaves behind all the thrills and bumps of a life well lived and a past that I can't forget. Most of my memories are pleasant; but many are not. There were, of course, the demons of my childhood, but in the last forty years, I also lost my mother, my brother, and two of my sisters. And after Jimmy died, I found myself far away from all the good friends who had made a mark in my life. It's a bittersweet feeling, as that roller-coaster slows, and you look around to see that all of those other guys you shared the ride with are now either gone or off on their own, watching their own rides come to an end.

On May 14, 1998, while working for the Yankees, I was informed that the old blue eyes Frank Sinatra died, and it made me realize that, in the end, no one escapes the rollercoaster's final stop.

The loss of a fatherly mentor and a loyal friend brought me back to the day I lost my father while the whole world mourned the loss of an icon. In New York, the lights at the Empire State Building were turned blue in his honor, and Las Vegas dimmed its lights, and all the casinos stopped operations for one minute in Frank's memory. At his funeral, thousands of mourners gathered to say goodbye to their beloved idol and the great humanitarian who always preferred to remain anonymous.

I remember how the legendary actor and Sinatra's close friend, Kirk Douglas, broke the sadness at Frank's funeral with his comment during his eulogy:

"Imagine now, Frank up there in Heaven, together again with his friends? Heaven will never be the same."

As my rollercoaster kept slowly rolling, certainly, there were more dark tunnels. One was when my daughter Effie narrowly escaped the 9/11 attacks at the World Trade Center, and the city that I loved fell into a deep grief of shock and pain. I wished that the thousands of others who lost their sons and daughters, brothers and sisters, uncles and cousins, had the same luck as I did that terrible day.

On June 3, 2001, I entered another dark tunnel when I learned that another good friend Anthony Quinn had died, and I drove to his house in Rhode Island to be with his family. With Tony, I'd always shared a very good friendship and also the pain of broken dreams.

Back in 1960, while filming one of his blockbuster movies *The Guns of Navarone* on the island of Rhodes, he fell in love with Greece and its people and bought a large seaside property with a dream to build a cultural center and a home to live there, but there was a flaw in his plans. He trusted the Greek government and his lawyers, who took his money and gave him nothing more than empty promises. All this time, my own dream to inherit some sentimental valuables from my parents had also turned into a nightmare, and we bonded over the same pain.

Those who have seen Quinn's portrayal of Zorba in *Zorba the Greek* certainly could see the deep connection he felt with Greece, but few knew how deep that connection ran. I remember him as a downtrodden man after the unstable Greek government denied his ownership because he was not a Greek citizen, a fact well-known prior the signing of the contracts of sale. Hundreds of thousands of dollars he had already spent were never returned with the excuse that "the case is still pending." He left New York and Hollywood, and with his family, he settled in a place that reminded him of his dream: Rhode Island.

I've seen both places and understood why Quinn must have seen similarities, but it was also in the names: the Island of Rhodes in Greece and the state of Rhode Island in America. He was so attached to his dream that, at his request, he was buried in the grounds of his newfound home in Rhode Island that reminded him so deeply of the home in his heart in Rhodes, Greece.

After his death, I kept visiting with his family, and during one of my visits, his widow, Katherine, asked me to examine a box with all the documents of Quinn's properties in Greece. It was all in Greek, and I took the box home with me. With my daughters, I started to look through it, and we soon discovered that all the contracts for sale of the property were signed and officially stamped, confirming clearly that Quinn was the rightful owner.

Armed with those documents, I returned to Greece again, but this time, with Quinn's family and a mission to find justice. But as Quinn once told me, "Finding justice within the Greek government is the real mission impossible."

When we arrived, we discovered that his properties in Rhodes had been developed into a tourist attraction called The Anthony Quinn Bay, which attracts thousands of tourists, who spend hundreds of thousands of euros that all went to a mayor of that region. We met with the mayor and presented him with Quinn's contracts, which he simply ignored, advising me of his intentions and hoping to intimidate me.

"Here, we operate the same way as the mafia operates in America," he told me, proudly.

I had seen enough mafia guys in my day to recognize that this guy was all talk, and his threats made me laugh. I realized that talking to him would accomplish nothing; however, I reciprocated with my own advice anyway.

"It is not wise to mimic and insult the mafia in such a way, as even they have rules that must be obeyed," I told him. But I don't think he understood what that meant.

Katherine and I didn't let up after that. We exposed the case to the Greek people through the television show hosted by journalist Makis Triantafyllopoulos, and it became clear that those properties should be turned over to the lawful landowner, the family of Anthony Quinn. But still the Greek government is reluctant to honor their contracts, and the case is still lingering in the courts, giving Greece a bad reputation in the eyes of the world and helping to spook any future investors.

Later, my rollercoaster would hit yet another sharp curve when on July 13, 2010, I learned that my good friend and longtime boss George Steinbrenner had died. That day, I took one more ride to the Bronx and visited the old stadium that was George's second home, where he singlehandedly built a Yankee dynasty and left a forty-one-year legacy that New York will cherish forever. There, he ran a tight ship with an iron fist, prompting some to call him a "heartless man."

I knew George Steinbrenner well, and I agree that he was a tough businessman; the sign on his desk clearly indicated that. But anyone who knew him understood that George was not a heartless man. Growing up on his father's chicken farm in Cleveland, Ohio, George was given chances and worked hard to become the owner of the Yankees, and he always wanted to give those same chances to others.

I remember one morning, we were going into the stadium, and security guys were trying to subdue a rowdy teenager who'd been caught spraying graffiti all over the building. George approached them and asked what the kid had done, but before the security guards could answer, the kid screamed at George, "Who the fuck are you?"

He looked at the kid straight in the eyes and told him, "I am the one who can keep you out of jail."

He then told the security guys to take him to the personnel office and ordered them to put him in a Yankee uniform and make him a ball boy, giving him a second chance. I remember seeing that kid, his jaw on the ground, eyes wide open, in clear disbelief from what he'd heard. It was like he was overwhelmed, not sure whether to be grateful or scared or happy.

"One more screw up from you, and you'll be out of here fast," George told that kid, and then he walked away.

George also gave second chances to a slew of others, never once caring about their background or past mistakes. It didn't matter if they were baseball superstars who had fallen, like Darryl Strawberry or Dwight Gooden, or a misguided kid from the Bronx. I also remember how George fought city hall, which wanted to relocate the run-down, city-owned stadium to a new location downtown with less capacity, but more luxury private boxes for the Wall Street honchos. However, George never forgot the hundreds of school kids from the Bronx who worked at the stadium every year during the summers, and he couldn't let them go without jobs, so he fought hard and won. The old stadium was renovated, and for thirty-three more years, it hosted countless championship games.

On April 2, 2009, the new Yankee Stadium that George built officially opened, and George celebrated it by taking one final lap around the field. At that point, he couldn't walk anymore, and so he boarded a Yankee mobile that drove him around as fifty-four thousand fans cheered him on. He was so proud of the Yankees and everything that he had built; he cried with happiness the whole way around and then passed the Yankee dynasty on to his two sons.

A few years later, I lost another friend, one who made a mark on my life. He had a magical singing voice, one that put smiles on the faces of frightened immigrants on their way to America. It was Elias, the young boy who I befriended while crossing the Atlantic on the boat called the *Italia*. We stayed friends for years after that, always updating each other on our adventures in our new country. And outside of my friends at Jimmy Weston's, Elias was one of my closest companions. His death brought down the final curtain on the clan that had become my family. Those were the good friends who captivated my life.

And I will always remember my uncle George who sponsored me to come to America. I will always remember all his kindness and wisdom, especially his advice "to learn English so I won't need a six-year-old as an interpreter just to buy a newspaper."

I will always be thankful to Uncle George.

He worked hard behind the scenes as a chef in the kitchen of a diner, but I remember that the hundreds of cars that filled Elizabeth Avenue for miles at his funeral procession showed what kind of a man he truly was.

I am also thankful to John and Fanny Pappas, the owners of Tempting Pies who gave me my first job in America and taught me my first words of English.

CHAPTER 40

Thank You, Friends

In telling my friends' stories in my book, I suppose the only thing I can do now is be true to their memory, to remember their perfections and their flaws together, to remember them as they wanted to be remembered. I will not say goodbye to them, but rather in sharing their memories, I offer them a heartfelt thank you because they took a broken young man from Greece and helped him find a home. And for that, I'll always be grateful.

Thank you to Audie Murphy, the hero soldier who gave so much so others could be free, and who gave me his friendship and his brotherly advice. He helped me learn the lessons I needed to learn as a young man establishing myself in the world.

After his death, I joined a national movement of veterans and fought hard for three years to convince the postal service and honor Audie Murphy with a postal stamp.

This was their argument: "We should not be reminding the people of wars."

"Heroes like Audie Murphy did not start the wars. They were the ones who finished them." That was our answer, and Murphy's postal stamp was finally unveiled. That was one of my greatest fights.

Speaking of fighters, I will always share with Muhammed Ali not only the feeling of being a stranger in our own hometowns, but also the ability to rise above.

Thank you to Anthony Quinn, who showed me true friendship and love for my country. In 2005, in his memory, I organized a book signing ceremony for his wife, Katherine's book about his life and art.

The event was held at the popular Terrace On The Park in Queens, and fans poured into the place to take one more glimpse of Quinn's work; I've always thought of it as my final thank you to my friend.

I frequently visit that new stadium that George built, and I feel his presence everywhere. It's in the walls, it's in the seats, it's in the smell of hot dogs and beer and cracker jacks, but mostly, it's in the roar of the crowd. Thank you, George.

I'll always be grateful to Frank Sinatra, for his kindness; he showed me the meaning of deep loyalty and friendship, and how such things can save your life. For Sinatra's one hundredth birthday, I produced seven concerts in theaters around New York, featuring Sinatra's many hit songs, as well as songs from his famous Rat Pack with entertainers from Las Vegas, such as Gary Anthony and Andy DiMino, both really talented entertainers who brought back all those wonderful moments of Frank and Dean. I had never produced anything before, but with the help of a friend with theater experience, Willy Mosquera, it was easy to be successful, and so many of Frank's and Dean's fans poured in.

But Sinatra is different from the rest, and I will never try to thank him because I know he would never accept it, and again would simply say: *"Lights out, Greek."*

I feel very fortunate to have lived in their times, to have had the privilege to get to know them, and to call them "my friends."

Of course, there are so many others that *impacted my life*. I hardly knew my father; my mother who showed strength and determination and turned difficult times into happy ones. My sisters and brothers-in-law Eleni and Costas, Marianthi and Christos, and Fredericka and Peter; my uncle George and aunt Eleni; my aunt Bebe and uncle Costas; my cousins and their families: Charlie and Jane, Gus and Catherine, Kimon and Carol; Patricia; Ernie and Cynthia; Peter and Joanne; Nick and Katherine; Nick and Mary; Christina and Mike; Ellie, Mimi, and Marica; the many Iatrous drawn together by Agnes Iatrou Reynolds-Russo; my nephews, nieces, and their families: Nick and Effie; Jim and Lidia; Jim and Chrissy; Patricia and John; Dennis and Ana; Chris; Konstantinos and Despoina; John and Helen; Demetri and Christina; Dean and Trinh; Mary and Marc; Millie and Morgan; my in-laws, the Kalogiannis family.

Good friends: Kathy Quinn and family (there are many good reasons that make me proud to consider you my friends); Bruce Robertson, thank you, friend; Anthony DeDona, a stand-up guy—I would never hesitate to walk anywhere with him next to me; the *other* Dino and Sophie; Paul and Kathy; Harry and Anna; Leonard and Mallory, my *rat pack* pals; Agia Markella; Katerina Lehou; King Willy Mosquera who was named by the *New York Daily News* as the *Nicest Guy in New York City;* Thompson; Bob Drury, both always there to lend a helping hand; Mickey who made watching football even more enjoyable; Al Sgambati, thanks for your support; and Vasilis and Anastasia; Chris and Anna Panopoulos and family; Carol Peck; Ted Andriotis; George Katisgiannis; Peter Scoufaras; Andreas and Vana Kontomerkos.

Thanks for Everything.
That's Amore.

My Grandson Leonidas, BRO#1

Me and BRO#1

Horsing around with BRO#1

BRO#1

My favorite songs:

"My Way"
"That's Life"
—Frank Sinatra

My favorite quotes:

*A real friend is the one who walks in, when
the rest of the world walks out.*
—Walter Winchell

A friend never gets in your way, unless you happen to be going down.
—Arnold H. Glasaw

Relatives come from inheritance; true friends come from love.
—Dino Pavlou

Don't count the days, make the days count.
—Muhammad Ali